IMAGES
of America

NORTH BREVARD
COUNTY

The home of George Webster Scobie was built in 1910. Members of the Scobie family can be seen here on the upstairs and downstairs porches. George was the son of William C. and Amelia Smith Scobie. Both were natives of Scotland. George was in the mercantile business with his father in Connecticut until he bought a 50-foot oyster boat in 1885 and set sail for Florida. Six weeks later he landed at Sand Point in Brevard County. Mr. Scobie was quite successful in the commercial fishing business. He built a barrel factory and shipped thousands of pounds of iced mullet by rail to northern markets. His fish houses were destroyed by the terrible fire of 1914, and his barrel factory burned in 1962.

IMAGES
of America

NORTH BREVARD COUNTY

John T. Manning, Ed.D.
and Robert H. Hudson

ARCADIA
PUBLISHING

Published by Arcadia Publishing
Charleston, South Carolina

Library of Congress Catalog Card Number: 99-65765

For all general information contact Arcadia Publishing at:
Telephone 843-853-2070
Fax 843-853-0044
E-mail sales@arcadiapublishing.com
For customer service and orders:
Toll-Free 1-888-313-2665

Visit us on the Internet at www.arcadiapublishing.com

CONTENTS

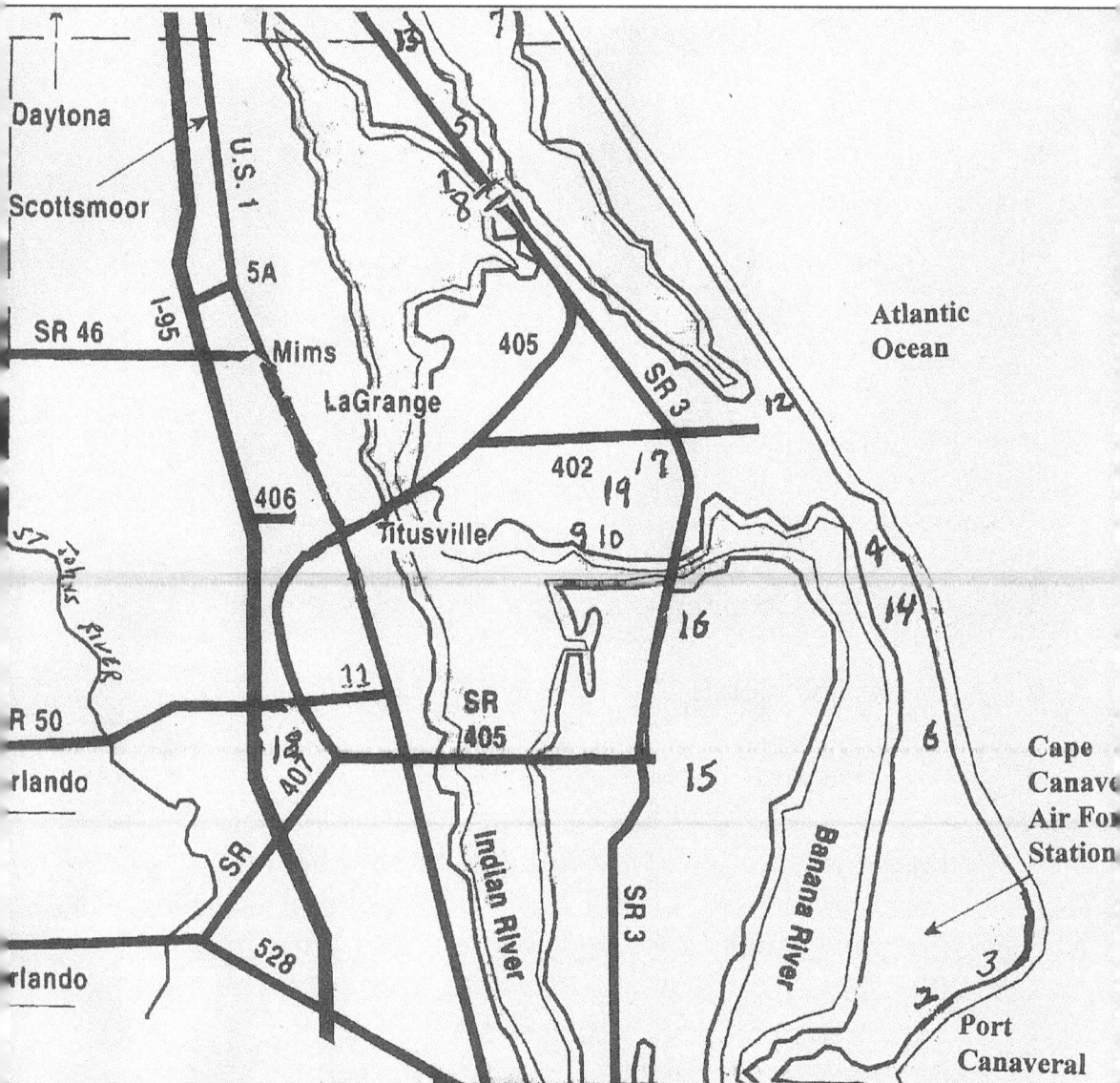

This is a composite map of Brevard County, north of Highway 528. It shows present and past cities, towns, communities, and places of interest. They are designated by number as follows: 1) Allenhurst; 2) Artesia; 3) Canaveral Beach; 4) Chester Shoals; 5) Clifton; 6) DeSota Beach; 7) Eldora; 8) Haulover; 9) Happy Creek; 10) Happy Hammock; 11) Indian River City; 12) Playalinda Beach; 13) Shiloh; 14) Titusville Beach; 15) the Kennedy Space Center; 16) Vertical Assembly Building; 17) Wilson; 18) the Windover Archeological Digs; and 19) Wisconsin Village. Prior to the federal government's take-over of the North Brevard area, visionaries had development plans for places that never quite materialized, including Satellite Estates, Myrtle Park Shoals, Paradise Bay, Dummitt Plantation Estates, Tween Seas Isle, Anna-Myrt Island, and Canaveral Harbor—The City of Romance.

INTRODUCTION

Brevard County, once owned by Spain, was claimed by the United States in 1821. It was part of St. Johns County until 1828, when Mosquito County was taken from St. Johns. Mosquito County encompassed an area bordered on the north by St. Johns County and on the south by Lake Okeechobee. In 1854, both Orange and Volusia Counties were formed from a part of Mosquito County. In 1855, Brevard County was taken from the northern part of what was to become, in 1858, St. Lucie County. Brevard County was named in honor of Judge Theodore Washington Brevard, who was comptroller of the state. The Sand Point District, an area of Volusia County, was taken in 1879 and added to northern Brevard. A post office was established at Sand Point, which now includes LaGrange and Titusville.

Much of Brevard, especially North Brevard, is fortunate to benefit from several bodies of water. To the west is the historical St. Johns River, which flows northward and provided a navigable waterway and a supply of freshwater fish. The river boats traveling the St. Johns brought early settlers and supplies to Brevard. On the east is the Indian River, which separates the mainland from Merritt Island. This river is very much a part of the Intracoastal Waterway and from pioneer days provided a means of transportation from settlement to settlement along the length of the county. Further to the east of Merritt Island is the Banana River, which separates Merritt Island from another low barrier island. This is the cape peninsular and was the eventual location of the missile center known as Cape Canaveral.

Citrus growing changed North Brevard from a hunting and fishing community into a stable productive agricultural economy that remained in place until the advent of the space age. First came the federal government's purchase in the 1950s of the land north of the port of Canaveral. It was here that the Cape Canaveral Missile Test Center was established. Later, as missile sizes increased and more land was needed for launch pads and fall-back areas, the Kennedy Space Center was created on North Merritt Island. It was this missile boom that really changed the area from the farm age to the missile age and stimulated the growth of the economy and the population.

Many towns, communities and homesteads disappeared as these governmental acquisitions of land forced residents to relocate. Hopefully, these photographs will serve as a reminder of "the way it was" in the vanished towns and communities, as well as in those that survive today.

ACKNOWLEDGMENTS

This book would not have been possible without the support and contributions of the following people:

Ann Brockett Ball, Ruth Barnhart, James Ball, Shirley Kyzer Barley, Wilma Mefford Bennett, Lyn Birnbaum, Susie Darden Brown, James Clark, the Tom Corbin-Indian River Masonic Lodge, John D'Albora, Jay Donnelly, Helen O'Flanagan Durian, Deette Feagan Foley, the Florida State Archives, the Fort Christmas Museum, George "Speedy" Harrell, Phyliss Stewart Herndon, Bob Kirk, Helen Scobie Kyzer, Saralyn Higgs Lamb, Jeanne Edwards Lyerly, Patricia Manning, Betty Mattingly, John Morley, Ada Edmiston Parrish, Betty Parrish, Ed Poe, Doris Porter, Roy Roberts, Mary Pritchard Schuster, Elizabeth Scobie, Lucy Mae Seigler, Waldene Snell, Robert Smith, the Tebeau-Field Library of Florida History, Joanna Waring Titcomb, Marge Threlkeld, Rose Wooley, Debra Wynne, and Barbara Ziegler.

In addition, numerous unnamed others suggested ideas and sources for pictures. Thank you all.

One

CITIES AND COMMUNITIES

In the infancy of Brevard County, LaGrange Community was the first social grouping of any consequence. David Nathaniel Carlile and his four sons were the core of LaGrange Community. Later, the Feaster, Gruber, Frensley, Cuyler and Kyzer families began to populate the area. From LaGrange, settlers spread throughout the area to form other settlements.

Britton J. Mims, a relative of the outlaw Jesse James, moved to the area and began the town of Mims. Unlike their cousin Jessie, the Mims family was law abiding and contributed greatly to the development of the area.

Titusville, formerly known as Sand Point, was born when soldier of fortune Colonel Henry Titus arrived in 1867 to take charge of a large tract of land owned by his wife, Mary Hopkins Titus, and her father.

Scottsmoor, a town at the extreme north end of the county, was once promoted as having the richest citrus land in Florida. It had its own railway station and was a major stop on Flagler's East Coast Railroad from Jacksonville to Miami.

Indian River City developed as a result of a land grant received by Joseph Delespine, who served the King of Spain and was rewarded with the Delespine Grant. Mary Boye, a relative of Delespine, inherited the grant. She and her husband, Captain James Pritchard, became major contributors to the growth of the North Brevard area. The Pritchards built a home one block north of Highway 50 on the Indian River.

Whispering Hills was formed around the Whispering Hills Golf Course west of Titusville and existed for several years before being annexed to Titusville.

The Brevard County Courthouse in Titusville was built in 1912 at a cost of $31,477 on land donated by Colonel and Mrs. Henry Titus. It replaced the original wooden courthouse. Three large wings were added in 1925 during the boom years. In the 1950s, when Cape Canaveral was chosen as the location for America's space program, a second building was constructed and connected by a walkway.

"From Sand Trails" aptly describes the beginning of Brevard County. In 1910, as on-lookers watch, workers level wagon ruts and apply shell to Wilson Avenue in Titusville. Eventually, it became the first paved street in the city.

"To Contrails" describes the progress that has been made in Brevard County, beginning with a small settlement called LaGrange in 1857, to the present, where missile contrails are visible as rockets blast off into space. No one could have foreseen that, in a few years, rocket launches into space would be visible from this primitive area.

On December 12, 1895, the city of Titusville was three fourths destroyed by a fire of unknown cause. Most of the buildings were made of wood and were quickly consumed by fire. However, to the benefit of the owners, a total of 17 iron safes survived the destructive fire and the contents were salvageable. The buildings of brick construction also survived. In the picture, the two-story building at the left is the Grandview Hotel. In the center is the Catholic church.

The Brady Grocery store opened in 1886. The business, founded by E.L. Brady, was moved to Titusville from LaGrange. Initially, the Titusville store was located on the southeast corner of Main Street and Washington Avenue, but the fire of 1895 destroyed that store. This two-story brick building was located on the corner of Julia Street and Washington Avenue.

Dr. Benjamin Rush Wilson was Titusville's first physician. He is shown here behind the counter of his drug store with his son, J.P. Wilson. Dr. Wilson was mayor and judge for several terms.

In 1908, R.W. Rhodes Clothier occupied the first floor of The Indian River Advocate building at the southwest corner of Washington Avenue and Julia Street. It was reported that, because of the vibrations, employees and customers would go outside once a week while the newspaper presses were running upstairs.

This view from Washington Avenue in the early 1890s looks east along Julia Street to the famous Hotel Dixie, located on the Indian River. To the left is the Indian River State Bank founded in 1888 and to the right Brady Grocery Store. Note the electric light poles, which were erected in 1890–91.

Capt. James Pritchard relaxes in front of his hardware store in Titusville. He was an entrepreneur who established and became president of the Indian River State Bank. He also opened a hardware store, and built the first electric light plant for Titusville.

In 1918 Pritchard Hardware was located on Washington Avenue in Titusville. Pictured here are, from left to right, D.B. Pritchard (with his daughter, Mary Pritchard Schuster), Ray Love, and Herman Shoup.

Shown here on the left is the C.H. Bethea Meat Market on Julia Street in 1925. The store was originally owned and built in 1912 by Mr. G.F. Duren. Sr. Mr. Bethea is at the left.

Electricity came to Titusville in 1890. This building, which is little more than a shack, housed the generators. Capt. James Pritchard was instrumental in building the first electric light plant, which was located behind the Pritchard Hardware store. At 12 midnight, a blink of the lights all over town was a signal—you'd better get home. Electricity was provided from early afternoon until midnight, when the lights were blinked to warn citizens that the plant would be shut down. On Saturday nights, when demand for electricity was high, the lights almost always failed, but the engineer at the plant would make adjustments to restore the lights. The plant was sold to Southern Utilities in 1914 and to the Florida Power and Light Company in 1926.

The Titusville Garage operated at the northwest corner of Washington Avenue and Main Street for several decades. Established in 1915, the garage was home to the Willis-Knight and Nash auto dealership as well as to Kelly tires. In time it became the Allied Chevrolet dealership and later still, the Gus Faulk Chevrolet dealership.

15

The W.G. Giles Sheet Iron and Plumbing Repair Shop pictured here in 1915 was built by Andrew Froscher as the first undertaking parlor in Titusville. Mr. Giles did many types of repairs, but his specialities were bicycles and plumbing. The building was located just north of today's city hall and across the street from the James Pritchard home.

This view of Washington Avenue was taken looking south in 1920. To the left are Pritchard Hardware and the Banner Drug Store; to the right are the Alpine Hotel, Losley Electric, and the Indian River Advocate building.

16

Yumies Store and Lunch Room in Mims was located next door to Dunn's Garage. According to the "Don't forget to vote" sign displayed, Yumies served as a precinct on this election day in the 1920s. Pictured here, from left to right, are Taylor Dunn (in the kiddie car), Mr. A.A. Dunn (Taylor's father), Jimmy Walker, unknown, and Wallace Feagan. Over the years, Yummies has been operated by Mrs. Koontz and her son, Mrs Nichols, Nina and Doctor Stanley, Lillie and Earl Harper, and Susie and Frank Kuebler. The building was torn down when U.S. Highway One was made four lanes.

Inside the Western Union Telegraph Office at 302 Washington Avenue are the following, from left to right: (sitting) W.H. Bell; (standing) Herbert Johnson Sr. and W.J. Pheil. In addition to serving the local area, this was a telegraph relay station between Miami and Jacksonville.

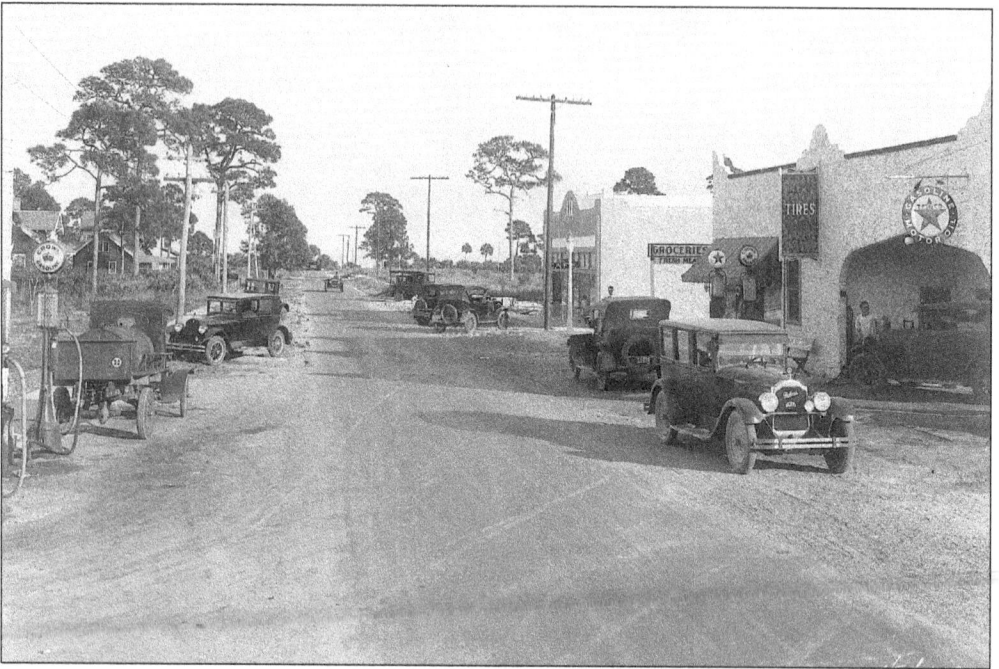

Indian River City is shown here in 1927 looking east along Coqunia Avenue toward the Indian River.

Indian River City lay at the intersection of Dixie Highway and State Road 50. In 1927 Clark's Corner was developed by Frank G. Clark. The "Dance Hall" was a popular hangout for local young people. No alcoholic beverages were sold. Indian River City was annexed to Titusville in the 1960s. The sign atop the garage points to "Orlando The City Beautiful."

The East Coast Lumber Company in Titusville was owned and operated by Leon Stewart, who is shown here in his 1928 Dodge automobile in the 1930s.

Titusville Volunteer Fire Department members are shown here in 1935 on Palm Avenue sitting on and standing beside an old Ward La France fire truck. Seated on the truck are Walter Giles and Hans Walker; the others are Dick Darden, Guy Sparkman, Dinky Brown, Guy Linder, Bedford Pirtle, Carl Boyd, Red Scrogan, Lee Baldwin, Ernie Brown, and Bill Knight.

The two uniformed officers are Police Chief A.J. Mefford and Assistant Chief Call Norwood (1891–1945). Mr. Norwood was a patrolman and chief of police. He also served in the Coast Guard. The two men would swap roles over the years.

Coca-Cola was first bottled in Titusville in 1916 by W.J. Darden. The bottling company took over the franchise and built this building on Washington Avenue in 1925. After the company moved production to Cocoa, the building was taken over by McCotter Motors, which occupied it until 1998.

20

The Indian River Masonic Lodge No. 90, Free and Accepted Masons was chartered on January 20, 1886, in Titusville, Florida. After losing their lodge building in a fire in 1915 they met in several buildings until this lodge was built in 1953. The principal motivator for building the lodge was E.B. Pirtle.

Florida Wonderland was a local tourist attraction situated at the intersection of Highway 50 and U.S. Route 1. It was built in 1960 by H.C. Kirk, who planted 1,500 palm trees along a jungle cruise waterway. There were exotic plants in a botanical garden, monkeys, alligators, lions, and an elephant. A narrow gauge railroad circled the park. Famous movie personalities were on hand to greet visitors.

21

This is the Jess Parrish Medical Center, which originated as the North Brevard District Hospital in 1957. It was a 28-bed facility in 1963 when the J.J. Parrish Sr. family donated a $100,000 piece of land on U.S. Route 1 in North Titusville as an expanded site for a new hospital. In June 1966, a new 7-story hospital (shown here) was opened. Plans are going forward in 1999 for a new hospital building.

Titusville decorated for Christmas in the 1950s. Pritchard Hardware, a landmark building, is on the left; Morley's Western Auto and Wisby's Jewelry Store is on the right. This view looks south on Washington Avenue.

Two

HOMES AND HOTELS

Pioneer residents coming to North Brevard usually made their first homes out of natural easily obtainable materials. The homes consisted of palmetto branches placed over wooden frames, similar to those used by the local Native Americans. However, by the mid-1800s more substantial materials were used and wooden homes began to make their first appearance.

Some of the early homes were built in the "Cracker" style, with open porches around the main structure. Generally, the kitchens were separate from the main building to lessen the chance of devastating fires. Later Queen Anne-style homes were built, along with Spanish architecture and even a Sears Roebuck home or two among the mix.

Col. Henry Titus arrived in Sand Point and built the Titus Hotel on the bank of the Indian River. Other early hotels were the Lund House on the Indian River and the Grandview Hotel, which was situated inland three blocks.

With the coming of the railroad down the East Coast and the construction of a passenger station at the west end of Julia Street, several hotels, apartments, and rooming houses sprang up along the street. Owners attempted to attract visitors before they reached the Titus House at the east end of Julia Street, four blocks away.

With the help of these hotels, Titusville became a tourist destination and might have been more of an attraction had railroad builder Henry Flagler been able to purchase property as he had hoped. Unable to purchase the desired property Flagler moved further south along the coast to Palm Beach and helped to build other counties.

Built by Capt. James Pritchard in 1891, this Queen Anne-style home is still one of Titusville's focal points. It is located on Washington Avenue at the corner of Pine Street and is occupied by Captain Pritchard's granddaughter, Mary Schuster. It was built of heart pine.

This is the oldest home still standing in Titusville. Built by Dr. Benjamin Rush Wilson in 1877, it was first located at the southwest corner of Hopkins Avenue and Orange Street, but was later moved to the southeast corner of Palm Avenue and Orange Street. The front porch has undergone extensive renovation.

Dummitt Castle, nestled between the Mosquito Lagoon and Indian River, sat in the middle of the oldest orange groves in Florida. Capt. Douglas D. Dummitt, a British subject, emigrated from Barbados in 1807. After first settling in St. Augustine, he moved to North Merritt Island, bringing with him bud wood stock from Spanish orange trees. The groves flourished and he shipped fruit to Port St. Augustine in canoes made from cypress logs. Dummitt's first home was little more than palmetto fronds attached to a pine frame, typical of the homes in the area. After Dummitt's death in 1872, Eicole Tamajo and his wife, who assumed the title of Duke and Duchess of Castellucio, purchased the groves. They built Dummitt's castle from heart pine and ships timbers salvaged from wrecks on the Canaveral coast. Legend has it that, because of marital problems, a wall was built through the center of the house and the two lived separately. The federal government took the land when the Kennedy Space Center was built in the 1950s, and the castle was moved to Titusville in the 1967. However, vandals burned it before it could be put to use as a museum.

This 1928 photo is of the home where *Star Advocate* newspaper publisher Henry Hudson and his family lived for 40 years. The design was influenced by Spanish architecture and the house was located on Washington Avenue in Titusville.

The Wager home at 621 Indian River Avenue was built in 1880 by Perry B. Wager, who came to Titusville in 1876 and with John W. Joyner opened a dry goods business at Sand Point. Perry had a flair for writing and a belief that the city needed a newspaper. He began Titusville's first newspaper by purchasing the newly founded *New Smyrna Florida Star* in 1880. He moved the printing equipment into the first floor of this home on the Indian River at the end of South Street. The second and third floors were added in 1890. For many years the second floor served as the town's opera house. One day Perry, his young son Ellis, and a colored field worker went to Happy Hammock to work the cane field. Perry told the others to go on, he would tie up the boat and bring the lunch basket shortly. When he didn't appear in the fields, the others went to look for him. Perry and the lunch basket had vanished. He was never heard from again.

The J.D. Cushman/Darden/McBride home on the left and the Scobie/Dr. H.J. Stevens/Guydette home on the right were built on Indian River Avenue in 1924.

The two-story Koon Funeral Home was constructed in the 1920s by James and Alma Koon, who had purchased it from the previous owner, Andrew Froscher. It was located on Palmetto Street and was sold to E.A. and Marie Smith, who operated it for many years until they sold it, and it became the North Brevard Funeral Home. The owners lived on the second floor.

The Bayview Apartment/Hotel, built about 1925, is of Spanish architecture and is located on the northwest corner of Washington Avenue and Sycamore Street. It was the first "home" of many veterans and their brides after World War II.

The Riverside apartment building was located just across the street from Titusville High School. It was replaced with a Howard Johnson's Restaurant.

The Pines Hotel was built in 1910 by the Titusville Fruit & Farm Lands Company at the intersection of Knox McRae Avenue and Mt. Vernon Street in Indian River City. It was the first hotel in Indian River City for winter tourists. The hotel's foundation is still visible.

Built by owner Bert Johnson in 1919 as an apartment hotel, the Pines was later converted to the Magnolia Theater. When movies became popular, it was renamed the Florida Theater. Currently, after major restoration, it is the Emma Parrish Playhouse.

The Hotel Arlington was located on Julia Street near the Florida East Coast Railroad Station. Here it is decorated for the 1912 July Fourth Celebration. It was also known as the Sterling Hotel and once was the home of Reverend T.A. Conway.

The Myers Cottage, located between Washington and Hopkins Avenue, was a popular two-story rooming house and dining room built at the turn of the 20th century. On this day in 1912, the house and automobile have been decorated for Titusville's July Fourth celebration.

The Palmhurst Hotel was one of several built on Julia Street early in the 1900s. It was a two-building complex with the rooms for visitors in the building shown here and the dining room and kitchen in a similar building to the right. No longer in use and deteriorating after the 1980s, a couple purchased it with the intent of starting a bed-and-breakfast. However, their plans failed, and the building was razed.

Located on busy Washington Avenue, the St. Charles Hotel was a two-story frame structure that offered spacious and airy rooms all opening onto the wide verandas that encircled the building. Constructed in about 1919, it was located on the site of today's law offices of Cianfronga, Telfer and Reda.

Scottsmoor Lodge was built in October of 1924 in Scottsmoor, the northernmost community in Brevard County. The lodge was a combined community center and hotel. It was used for entertaining tourists and community gatherings. There were 25 sleeping rooms. It had hot and cold running water, showers, bath tubs, and electric lights. There was a full kitchen and a dining hall that could seat 400 people.

The Oleander Inn on Coquina Avenue in Indian River City, built in the 1920s, was a popular residential building with many apartments. It was later known as the Scapa Hotel.

Shown here is a 1932 view of the three-story Hotel Dixie. It was constructed in 1890 on the former site of the Titus House, which was built in 1870 on the Indian River. A popular destination and stopover for tourists for many decades, it was was also a meeting place for local people to enjoy club and social activities. The hotel burned in 1962. The Federal Housing and Urban Development Building, Titusville Towers, is now located on the site.

Three

CHURCHES AND SCHOOLS

A rudimentary church building was erected from logs and thatched with palmetto fronds shortly after the first settlers arrived in LaGrange. LaGrange was the first community in Mosquito, later named Brevard County. All denominations shared the services. People came early and stayed late because many had traveled long distances to attend all day services. They came because they had been raised in traditional church families, and also because it was the only social event available to them, living in a wilderness as they did. They came early to catch up on news, to trade with each other, and to participate in activities, such as horse racing. From the first simple structures grew the more elaborate edifices that we see in the cities today. Along with the churches came the schools. Often, churches and schools shared the same building, as was the case in LaGrange.

This is a 1927 view of St. Gabriel's Episcopal Church in Titusville. It was built in 1887 on land that was donated by two people, Mrs. Mary Evalina Hopkins Titus, wife of Colonel Henry Titus, and J. Dunlin Perkinson, a lay reader. Originally, the church was named St. Johns; however, the name was changed to St. Gabriel's in response to the gift of a special St. Gabriel's stained glass window. Also, there is an unusual "lighthouse" window honoring Captain Mills Olcott Burnham, who was the first Cape Canaveral Lighthouse keeper. The bell was installed in 1892.

LaGrange is a community in North Brevard County. It is a microcosm of all that went into forming the United States. The hardships and dangers confronting the early pioneers of LaGrange were no less than those faced by early settlers in other parts of the United States. Everything that the community of LaGrange was, is represented in this picturesque church located on Old Dixie Highway, just north of Titusville. The LaGrange Church, begun in 1869, is the oldest church between New Smyrna Beach and Key West and the oldest Protestant church between St. Augustine and Key West. Originally built of logs, the church was rebuilt with lumber in 1894 and dedicated by the Reverend William N. Chaudoin. LaGrange Church was the social center for the early settlers. Non-denominational religious services were conducted for various faiths. There were all-day meetings with dinner served on the grounds. Families came from long distances on foot, by boat, on horseback, and by carriage.

Some of the first settlers in Brevard County, who erected LaGrange Church, are named in this stained glass window. Jacob Norris Feaster and his brother, John Christopher Columbus Feaster, were pioneers of North Brevard. They came here from Feasterville, South Carolina, in 1867 and settled at LaGrange with a sister and an uncle. Britton Jones Mims moved to the area from Georgia. It was from his family that the city of Mims derived its name. "Uncle" Tom Johnson (Cockshutt) taught at night without compensation, using his log cooper (barrel) shop as a classroom. It was the first classroom in Brevard County. He also taught Sunday school at LaGrange for 47 years. His surname was Cockshutt, but he used the name Johnson because Cockshutt was objectionable. William Shackleford Norwood was born in Georgia, served in the Confederate Army, and married a Feaster. He started the first mail route in Brevard and eventually served in both the local and state government. Robert Morris Singleton was a respected physician who came to Brevard from Opelousas, Louisiana. William Perry Day moved to the area from Valdosta, Georgia.

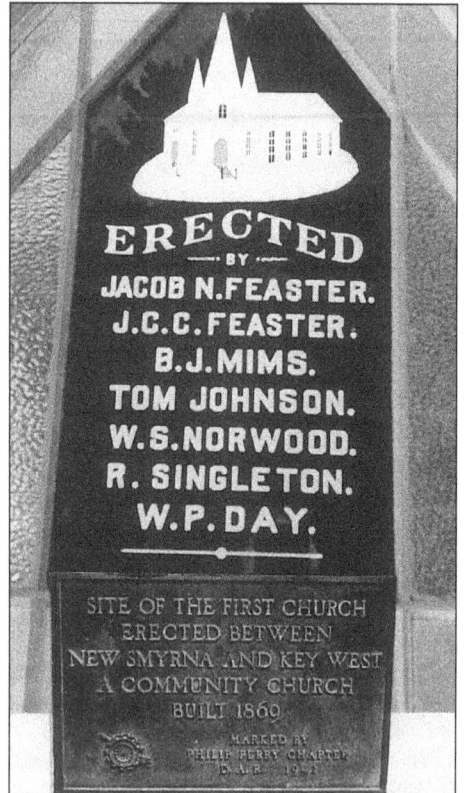

ERECTED
— BY —
JACOB N. FEASTER.
J. C. C. FEASTER.
B. J. MIMS.
TOM JOHNSON.
W. S. NORWOOD.
R. SINGLETON.
W. P. DAY.

SITE OF THE FIRST CHURCH
ERECTED BETWEEN
NEW SMYRNA AND KEY WEST
A COMMUNITY CHURCH
BUILT 1869

MARKED BY
PHILIP PERRY CHAPTER
D. A. R. 19??

The First Baptist Church of Titusville was founded May 19, 1889. Rev. A.D. Cohen led the erection of the First House of Worship in 1892 on Palm Avenue. The new church was built on the corner of Main Street and Hopkins Avenue in 1955. Four preachers from this church served in the chaplaincy of the Armed Forces from Titusville. Robert Ripley featured an item, "The Four Chaplains From The Same Church," in his famous column. The chaplains were Marshall Mines, James Sutherland, James T. Mashburn, and Loys Frick.

This modest wooden structure, pictured in 1939, represented the Catholic Church, which is now known as St. Teresa's. It has evolved into the present-day complex of church, office, rectory, and school. Father John O'Boyle, originally from Donegal County, Ireland, arrived in Titusville in 1886 and began ministering to Catholics in the area. The original frame church stood at the corner of Hopkins and Orange Avenues. A second church was built at Hopkins Avenue and South Street in 1937 by Father Hegarty. The present church property at Hopkins Avenue and Ojibway Street was purchased in 1955.

A dedication was held in 1981 to commend the restoration of the bell to the Bethlehem Baptist Church. Here, Deacon Harris points to the plaque while his wife, Eleanor, and Pastor D. Grooms look on.

The Mims Methodist Church was built in 1889. The lumber came from a sawmill near LaGrange, and the labor to build the church was donated by its members. The church was dedicated in 1892 with a program and dinner on the grounds. Circuit rider preachers held services until the congregation was able to support a full-time preacher. To favor the women who had to prepare and serve Sunday dinner, extra noon services were held for both Sunday school and church services.

PROGRAM

Of the First Setting of the
Church's Aid and Building Convention of Florida
to Convene with the
ST. JAMES BAPTIST CHURCH, — MIMS, FLORIDA.
AUGUST 23 — 26, 1928
Rev. A. L. Freemon, Pastor.

Thursday Night Local Program .... By St. James Baptist Church and Choir
Open ing   Song .... By the choir
Invocation .... Deacon   E. G. Grant
Scripture Lesson
Song .... Choir
Opening Remarks .... by the Pastor
Reading .... Miss Luella Campbell
Welcome In Behalf of City .... Mr. J. Warren
Welcome In Behalf of St. James Baptist Church .... Deacon S. A. Mitchell
Sextette .... St. James Choral Class
Welcome In Behalf of Womens Home Mission .... Mrs. Mattie Mitchell
Solo .... Miss Eliza James
Welcome In Behalf A. M. E. Church .... Rev. Elmore
Welcome In Behalf Primitive Baptist Church .... Rev. Frasier
Solo .... Miss Elizabeth Warren
Reading .... Miss Queen Esther Abrahams
Paper .... Mrs. S. M. Moye
Selection .... Young Girls Circle
Welcome In Behalf of Fraternal Orders .... Mrs. Jerry Zeigler
Welcome In Behalf of Business Men .... Mr. S. M. Moye
Solo .... Mrs. A. L. Freemon
Collection .... Assigning Delegates
Adjournment
FRIDAY MORNING AUGUST 24TH
10:—10:15 Song Service .... Convention Choir
10 15—10:30 Devotion .... Conducted by Messenger of New Smyrna
10:30—10:45 Talk by The President .... Rev. S. L. Johnson
11:00 A. M. Introductory Sermon .... Rev. J. W. Small
Alternate .... Rev. Moore
Song .... Convention Choir
Collection—Enrollment—Appointing of Committees—Adjournment
Friday 2:00 Song Service .... Convention Choir
2:30 Presidents Address .... Rev. S. L. Johnson
3:00 Sermon .... Rev. J. D. Walker
Alternate .... Rev. Greene
Collection—Enrollment
4:00 Bible Institute .... Rev. K. D. Reddick
Song .... Choir
Report of Committees—Election of Officers—Adjournment
Friday 8:00 P. M. Song Service .... St. James Choir
Invocation .... Rev. J. Mitchell
8:30 Doctrinal Sermon .... Rev. J. W. Driskol
Alternate .... Rev. Terrie
Solo .... Miss Grace Campbell
Collection—Adjournment
SATURDAY, AUGUST 25TH WOMEN'S DAY
10:—10:15 Song .... Convention Choir
10:15—10:30 Devotion Conducted by .... Messenger Daytona
11:00 A. M. Missionary Sermon .... Rev. R. J. Taylor
Alternate .... Rev. J. E. Hawkins
Instrumental Solo .... Miss Gilbert, Titusville
Appoi   nt of Committees—Collection—Enrollment—Adjournment
2:00—2:15 D   on Conducted by .... Messenger Titusville
2:15—2:30   sson Taught by Moderator .... Rev. R. W. Lawrence
3:00—3:30 I   ng .... Rev. J. D. Taylor
Alternate .... Rev. Greene of Gifford
Collection—Enrollment—Report of Officers
4:30 Presidents Address — Election of Officers
— Adjournment —
Saturday 8:00 P. M. Devotion Conducted by .... Messenger of Gifford
8:30 Evangelistic Service Conducted by .... Missionary M. Dinkins
Duet .... Mrs. Mamie Sims and Mr. Chezzie Jackson
Collection—Enrollment—Adjournment
SUNDAY MORNING, AUGUST 26TH, JOINT SESSION
9:30 Model S. S. Conducted by .... Bro. Terrie
11:00 A. M. Song Service .... St. James Choir
Educational Sermon .... Rev. R. W. Lawrence
Alternate .... Rev. Williams
Solo .... Mrs. M. Mitchell
Collection—Adjournment
2:00 P. M. Devotion by .... St. James
Invocation
Song .... Choir St. James
2:30 Sermon .... Rev. H. R. McDonald
Alternate .... Rev. W. M. E. Gilbert
Collection—Adjournment
6:00 P. M. Model B. Y. P. U. Conducted by .... J. D. Lawrence
8:00—8:15 Song Service .... Choir St. James
Invocation .... Deacon H. B. Baggs
Solo .... Mrs. Evelyn Hall
8:30 Annual Sermon .... Rev. A. L. Freemon
Reading .... Miss Mamie Sims
Solo .... Mrs. A. L. Freemon
Collection—Contest—Adjournment

This 1928 program lists the activities and the members of the St James Baptist Church who helped host this important event.

The original Mims Baptist Church was founded in 1912, and the first pastor was Reverend W. B. Kyzer. The church building was completed in 1928. This picture was taken in 1938, and show members and guests gathered for an annual picnic. The pastor was Robert Kicklighter, who was attending nearby Stetson University. Once a year, the church observed a Stetson Day. Among those pictured here are the following: Eva Taylor, B.I. Ricard, Frank Sims, Lester Cantrell, Chet Lybrand, Rena Sims, Alice Sharpe, Ralph Sharpe, Andrew Sharpe, Ellen Burkett, Enid Taylor, Pearl Marr, Mrs. Alewyne, Virginia Dunn, Margaret Marr, Mary Steele, Eola Kyzer, Wilma Barrs, Marjorie Folsom, and Winfried Folsom.

Pictured here are members of the former St James Baptist Church of Mims prior to 1964. Reverend James A. Massey (standing), was the pastor of both St James and Greater St James Missionary Baptist Church for 31 years. Members seated here, from left to right, are as follows: (front row) Daisy Harris, Ada Seigler, Florine Hatfield, Mother Mamie King Bell, and Deacon Eugene Abrams; (second row) Deacons Ezekiel Grant Jr, Fuller S. Seigler, Minnie Grant, Melvin Claire, Lisa Shelton, and Deacon H. J. Strickland. The little girl kneeling is Martha Jean Stroman Allen, daughter of Earl and Grace Stroman, who was raised by the Mamie King Bell family and their daughter Lucy Mae Bell Seigler.

The First Presbyterian Church was "born" on a steamboat on the Indian River in 1886. A steamboat captain placed a plate on a table in the ladies cabin of the boat with a card that read that there was no church in Titusville. Thus, donations were solicited. In less than six months, the church was built and furnished. The first service was held on January 2, 1887, at the Titus Hotel. The church, as shown here, was built later that year at the southwest corner of Hopkins Avenue and Pine Street. In 1967, the building was sold and a new structure was built at the corner of Golfview Drive and Park Avenue.

Titusville First Methodist Church was organized as a mission circuit in 1875, and the first pastor was A.A. Barnett. The original church was built on the north side of Orange Street in 1889. The church was moved in 1903 to the corner of Main Street and Hopkins Avenue. It was moved again to the corner of Palm Avenue and Main Street. The present church was built at the corner of Palm and Broad Streets in 1954.

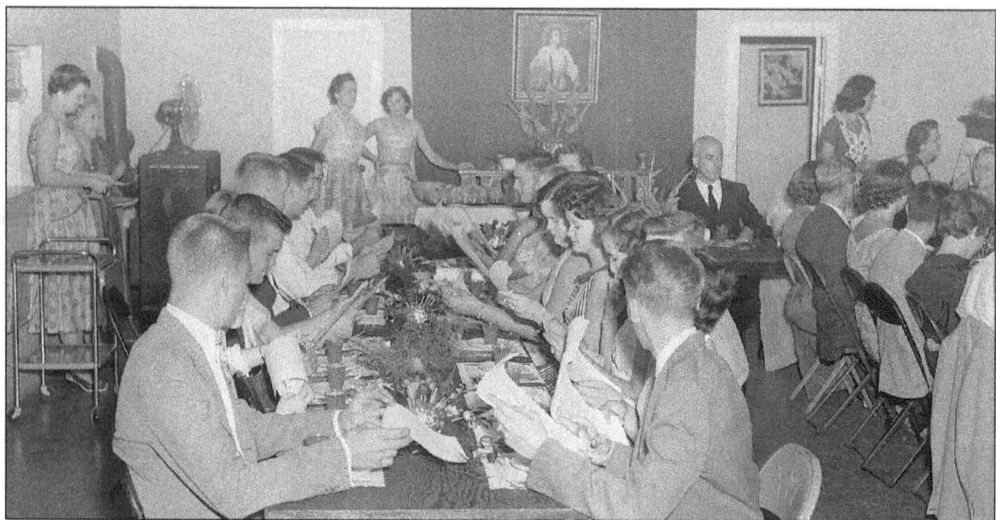

The First United Methodist Church of Titusville has a long tradition of honoring all the young church members that graduate from local high schools. Here, at Hennessy Hall, the Class of 1956 is honored at a banquet. Hosting the event and pictured here are, from left to right, as follows: (standing) Grace Wattwood, Mamie Love, Martha Salter, Susie Brown, Alverda Howell, and Violet Griffin; (students on the left side of the table) Earl Futch, Jim Schuster, Jimmy Wells, and Jackie Pauley; (students on the right side of the table) Betty McCushey, Bertha Glisson, Ann Draa, and Larry Morgan.

In 1926, The LaGrange School consisted of one classroom and one teacher. From left to right are as follows: (front row) Margaret Carlile, Alice Hickman, Lynie Earl Finney, Tom Frensley, Olga Finney, Elaine Waring, Ruby Roberts, and Lucile Roberts; (second row) Lucile Metzker, Burrell Ives, John Frensley, Lavina Frensley, Joann Waring, Earl Hickman, Frank Puckett, Everitt Simmons, and Virgil Simmons; (third row) Elamae Carlile, Hattie Hudson, and Elsie Hickman.

The Titusville Negro School faculty of 1936–37 is pictured here. From left to right, they are as follows: Walter Wynn, Bernice McDowell, Sadye Gibson, Naomi Wynn, Wihelmenia Gilbert, Victoria Rogers, and Principal Harry T. Moore. Principal Moore, who displeased the white establishment by registering African-Americans to vote, was later fired by the Brevard County School Board. For the same reason, he and his wife were murdered in a 1952 bombing that still remains unsolved.

Three members of the July 1985 Negro School Reunion reminisce. On the left is Mrs. Connie Gibson Williams, Class of 1915. Next is Mr. W.A. Mace, Class of 1915 and Mrs. Elvira Geraldine Brown, Class of 1916. Mrs. Brown is the granddaughter of the schools namesake, Andrew Gibson.

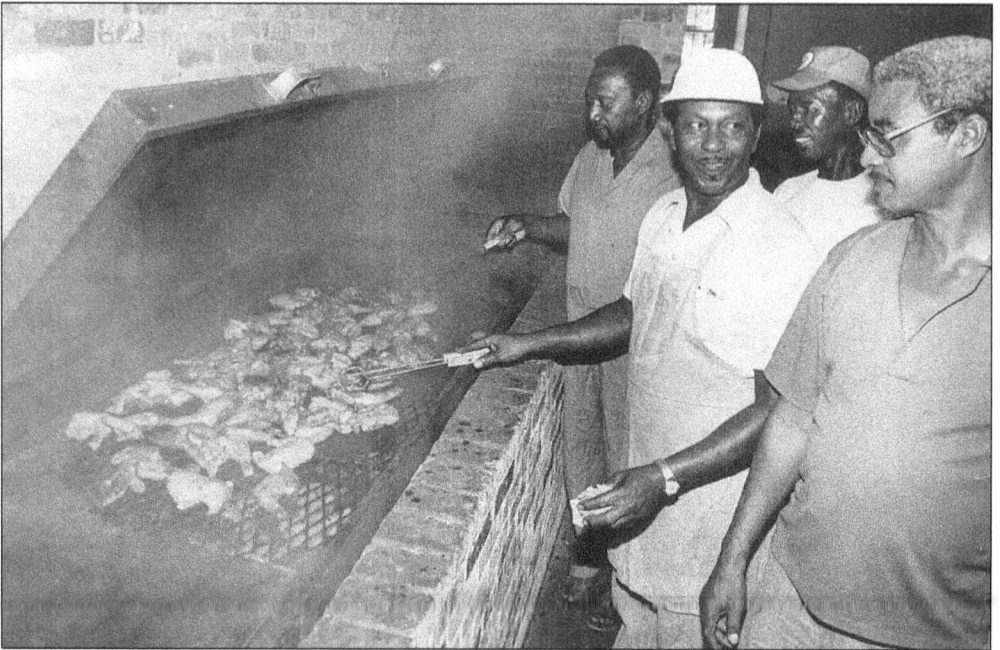

Four men prepare food at the Negro School Reunion, held in 1985 at Fox Lake Park. They represent their classes as follows, from left to right: Lorenzo Wright (Class of 1950), Fred Banks (Class of 1952), Amos Bell (Class of 1951), and Curly Edmonson (Class of 1953).

Here is a 1906 view of the Titusville School, built in the late 1800s on Washington Avenue for all grades through 12. In 1917, the building was moved to Wager Street and became the Titusville Negro School. It was replaced on this site by a three-story concrete building, also occupied by all 12 grades. It later became Titusville Elementary before being torn down to make way for Titusville City Hall.

The fifth grade class at Titusville Elementary School in 1930, are as shown, from left to right: (front row) Rosa Wager, Ruby Burke, Lillian Morgan, Stella English, and Morey; (middle row) Edward Poe, Lewis Fresh, Richard Davis, John McPherson, Dick Flood, Percy Hilliard, and Pat Flood; (top row) Stacy Turner, Bedford Pirtle, Raleigh Anderson, Douglas Barnhart, Hubert Ennis, Pete Metzer, and Helen Quinn (teacher).

These are teachers and their students who graduated from The Titusville School after the 1910–11 school year. The following teachers are seen here, from left to right: Susie Lecter, Susan Gladwin, Ruth Farley, Carrie Mendel, Gertrude Mendel, and Mr. Simmons, standing at the rear.

Pictured here is a class play at Titusville Elementary School in 1925. Pictured are, from left to right, as follows: (top row) Sarah Ferguson, Marion Linder, Jane Shehee, Virginia Rhea Love, Ann Elizabeth Brockett, unknown, unknown, unknown, Jean Clark, unknown, unknown, Virgil Conklin, Genevive Everitt, Truman Grammell, Mary Pritchard, Frances Clark, Grace Morgan, and Nona Koontz; (bottom row) Nellie Enright, Lola Allen Osban, Hattie Hudson, Woodrow Darden, Robert Conderman, Edward Poe, Clyde Pirtle, Claude Pirtle, Norman Botsford, unknown, Ruth Nelson, Rosa Wager, and Howard Threlkeld.

Graduating in the middle of World War II, a very grim time for the United Sates, these students can still smile in expectation of the life ahead for them. Pictured here are students in the Titusville High School Graduating Class of 1943. From left to right are as follows: (front row) Wiona Brooks, Ethel Ray, Carolyn Taylor, Betty Poe, Elaine Waring, and Lora Shoup; (second row) Lulu Etta Green, Lillian Louise Roberts, Elizabeth Sue Holland, Bertie Granger, Ruth Bethea, and Frances Parker; (third row) Florence Folsom, Jean Helms, Ann Bruner, and Allison Hendrix; (fourth row) Buster Jones, William Higginbotham, Joe Lee Walker, and Joe Cushman.

44

The high school homecoming dance was an annual event to honor the most popular couple chosen as king and queen of homecoming. Here, staged in the Titusville gymnasium (now Badcock Furniture Store), are the 1954 king and queen with their entourage. From left to right are as follows: Meredith Jorden, Alan Publin, Mary Lou Conway, Junior Crow, Glen Higgs, Betsy Jones, Mary Lee Feagan, Queen Ruth Bell, King Linville Brown, Wayne Brown, Betty Mitchell, and Jack Pauley.

Officers of the 1958–59 Titusville High School Band gather to go over plans for another marching event. Those pictured here, from left to right, are as follows: Mona Lee, Katherine Johns, Julius Robinson (band captain), and Eddie Benzenhafer.

This is the first grade classroom at the new Mims Elementary School in 1967. Pictured here are, from left to right, as follows: (first row) Jeffery Wright, Carolyn Lay, Lee Meserve, Mary Kimble, and Carolyn Anderson; (second row) Lori Parker, David Arriett, Jessie Touchton, Donna Johnson, and Jonathan Fluharty; (third row) Donna Bolton, Stephen Bloss, David Parker, Leslie Polk, and Michelle Penley; (fourth row) Allan Duff, Pat Flanagan, Beth Lynn, Tammy Mullins, and Alison McArty; (fifth row) Richard Williams, Duane McDaniel, Diane Sands, and Jimmy Swindle. Standing at the rear are Susan Jenkins and Donald Floyd. The teacher, Dr. Patricia C. Manning, is known today as professor emeritus at the University of Central Florida.

Here is the 1981–82 class picture at Riverview Elementary School in Titusville. The teachers are at the far right and are, from left to right, as follows: (standing) Effie Clifford, Betty Green, and Lucy Mae Seigler.

46

This concrete two-story version of Mims Elementary School, built in 1917, is a far cry from the first school structure. Originally, when the school reached the target of ten students, the board of education erected a one-room schoolhouse. The school was built high above the ground, and wild hogs rooted underneath. Hogs carried fleas, which infested the school. A smoldering fire was started beneath the building to kill the fleas. The fire got out of control and destroyed the building, the first two-story building in the city. The present Mims Elementary School is located on the same site near U. S. Highway 1.

The graduating class of the eighth grade at Mims School in 1927 is shown here. Pictured here are, from left to right, as follows: (front row) Sarah Selina Roberts, Keatly Nicholson, Lyle Duff, and Barbara Jones: (back row) Gladys Roberts, Eleanor Green, Principal J. D. Pepper, Evelyn Baggett, and Sadie Gibbs. The students attended Titusville High School the following year.

This horse-drawn school bus, pictured in 1906, was the first in Brevard County, and it provided transportation for students attending Titusville's one-room school. Pictured here are, from left to right, as follows: Marian Gruber (Mrs. Marian Barnhart), Bertha Frazier (Mrs. Ed. Miller), Winnie Johnson, Nainie Frazier (Mrs. Fred Frensley), and Lucian Nail. Gifford Kittles is the driver standing by the wagon. The girl on the horse is Louise Curtis Waring, who became a silent screen star and the mother of Champ Waring, Joanna Titcomb, Lois Ramage, and Elaine Vaughn.

School bus drivers, Ethel and Carl Battle, are shown here with students and parents in 1918. The couple drove buses for 30 years. They brought children to Titusville from Mims and Indian River City. Both the Battles were independent contractors with the Brevard County School System. The first buses did not have sides, and when it rained, the students had to lower the canvas sides. The buses were custom-made in Daytona.

48

This school started its existence as the Titusville School and was for all grades, until the name was changed to The Bay View Elementary School in 1901. It was located at the current city hall site on Washington Avenue. Miss. Carrie Mendel, teacher of these third and fourth grade students, taught for several decades, never married, and lived to be 103. Mendel Avenue in Titusville is named for her.

The first Titusville School began in 1888 and was located on Main Street. It was destroyed by fire and was rebuilt on Washington Avenue. Here, children of all grades are shown with teachers and some proud parents.

The members of the Titusville High School faculty of 1955–1956 are pictured here, from left to right, as follows: (front row) Marion McLester, William Buntin, Frances Louwerse, Elizabeth Adams, Cody Copeland, Becky Hulbert Sharpe, John Littlechild, and Principal Bill Weeks; (back row) Murray Swan, Craig Morgan, Joe Langston, Roger Shepard, Barney Price, Mack Haynes, Jim Bryson, and Leslie Sparks.

Mr. Rhodell Murray, the master of ceremonies for the Titusville Negro School Reunion, unveils a temporary plaque at the July 1985 ceremony dedicating the Social Service Center in memory of the slain Civil Rights leader Harry T. Moore. Here is a quote about the school: "Titusville Negro School: Following temporary sites on Washington Avenue in 1883 and on Dummitt avenue in 1886, Titusville Negro School was located on this site in 1915. It housed grades 1-8. The original building was burned in 1931, and a new 8 classroom frame building was erected. An auditorium was added later. The school grew to 12 grades, and the first high school class was graduated in 1938. After the new Andrew J. Gibson school was opened in 1957, this site was abandoned and the old building razed."

RIVERVIEW ELEMENTARY
1979-1980

Riverview Elementary School, at Titusville, Florida, first opened in 1970. The first principal was Babe Scarborough. The 1979–80 faculty is shown here. Members are, from left to right, as follows: (front row) unknown, Marty Murphy, Jim Connover, Linda Briggs, Cliff Estes, Jerry Beverly, Lucy Seigler, Connie Hyder, Alice Graves, and Jean Sanders; (second row) unknown, Betty Green, Jane Miller, Marion Towne, Gail Fishwater Perdoma, Clyde Talley, unknown, and Kathy Bryant; (third row) Nora Redding, Effie Clifford, Nell Prouse, Kathy Murray, unknown, Nancy Dickinson, Harlie DePersia, Brenda Graham, Susie Cross, Linda Wittersheim, Joyce Harris, and Bertha Hickman; (fourth row) Terry Lee, Phyllis Porter, unknown, Denise Roberts, Donna Mays, Jerry Moore, Helen Crotteau, and Joe Gregory.

Pictured above in 1924 are students and teachers of the Titusville School on Washington Avenue. The school was constructed in 1916–17 and was the first school to be built of concrete. It was constructed on the site of the former two-story wooden school building. The new building housed all 12 grades. It contained 20 classrooms, a cafeteria in the basement, an auditorium,

and a third-floor gymnasium. It served the North Brevard area as a school for both elementary and secondary students until a new building was completed in 1927. After 1927 it was named Titusville Elementary, and eventually it became Bayview Elementary. The building was torn down in 1972, and Titusville City Hall was built on the site.

In 1926, the first Titusville school orchestra was formed with Bernice Conquist as director. Pictured here, from left to right, are as follows: (front row) Jack Olmstead, Leroy Kimble, unknown, Marie Boye, Helen Scobie, and Ellen Brown; (back row) unknown, Arlie Brockett, Sam Holmes, Bernice Conquist, Walter Kimble, Homer Conkling, and Susie Darden. Members absent were Madison Koetz and Augusta Bradford.

The first building devoted solely to high school classes in Titusville was this Spanish-style structure in what was then South Titusville (pictured in 1927). The building featured terrazzo floors, glazed brick halls, a large second-floor library, and one-story wings housing industrial arts and home economics departments and a cafeteria. Over the entrance was a bell tower, which was reproduced in smaller form when the school was torn down in 1972. A more modern Titusville High campus occupies the site.

Four

PEOPLE OF NOTE

Professional football stars, actors and actresses, a politician, a war criminal, a former slave, segregation fighters, and others who lived or passed through North Brevard are among the area's people of note. Leading the group is pioneer settler Colonel Henry Titus, the father of Titusville, who staked his chances on a game of dominoes to name the city after himself. A former U.S. vice-president and Confederate treasurer came this way. Doctors, a lighthouse keeper, a native of Bavaria, pioneer residents, five court clerks (who together served 105 years), club members, and lodge members all combined to make North Brevard a more interesting place to live, work, and visit.

These five men served Brevard County for a total of 105 years as clerks of the circuit court. They are, from left to right, as follows: (top row) A.A. Stewart (for 40 years from 1871 to 1912), J. F. Mitchell (for 8 years from 1913 to 1921), and Norris T. Froscher (for 11 years from 1921 to 1932); (bottom row) G.M. Simmons (for 30 years from 1932 to 1962), and Curtis Barnes (for 14 years from 1962 to 1976).

Colonel Henry Titus, founder of Titusville, was born February 13, 1823, in Trenton, New Jersey. He married Mary Hopkins of Georgia. Colonel Titus, because of his many escapades prior to arriving in Titusville, was sometimes referred to as a soldier of fortune. Reported to be in favor of slavery, in 1854, he went to Kansas to oppose John Brown and became involved in the "Kansas Troubles" and was captured by abolitionists. He was captured again in Nicaragua while taking part in a revolution there. He served as Adjutant General of Pennsylvania and acquired the title of Colonel. During the Civil War, he served as a blockade runner for the Confederacy. Eventually, Colonel Titus, with his family, settled at Sand Point, a refuge for his contraband dealings.

Later, while he served as postmaster, he won a domino game where the stakes were his right to change the name of the town from Sand Point to Titusville. Because of Colonel Titus's effort in 1880, Titusville was named the county seat of Brevard. The Colonel and his wife were very generous and donated land for churches and for government buildings. He also built Titus House, a tropical-style hotel, which was later incorporated into the Dixie Hotel.

Due to illness late in life, he spent long hours confined to a wheelchair. One of his sons reported "that Colonel Titus sat on the front porch facing Washington Avenue with a rawhide whip (that he once used to drive cattle in Texas) and that chickens, dogs, pigs, and pickannies had better pass with caution." Colonel Titus died in 1881 at age 59.

56

Andrew Gibson, who was born in 1830 into slavery in Georgia, was married to Miss Miley Macon. He, his wife, their first daughter Emily, and his brother Edward made Titusville their home in 1873. Mr. Gibson was the first black businessman to open a restaurant for both blacks and whites. He served as a jailer for the city of Titusville. He was a barber and ran a shoe repair shop. He and his brother Edward bought a church building, where he served as a deacon until his death in 1928. The Titusville High School for Negroes was named for him in 1928. It is known today as the Gibson Center.

John Cabell Breckinridge, a war criminal who was wanted dead or alive by the United States, made his escape from the federal army by way of LaGrange in Brevard County. Breckinridge, once the 14th vice-president of the United States, ran on a pro-slavery ticket for president against Abraham Lincoln. He joined the Confederacy to protect his slave interests and became secretary of war and treasurer under Confederate President Jefferson Davis. As he made his escape from Richmond, and he carried the remains of the Confederate treasury. He traveled down the St. Johns River to Carlile's Landing (LaGrange) and, after a few days with local help, carried his boat over to the Indian River, where he headed south and eventually escaped to Europe.

Pictured here is the So-So Club of 1936, which alternated meeting places each month. Here, they are meeting at the home of Edna Roberts at Orsino, Merritt Island. It began as a sewing club and then became a social club that is still in existence today. The seated child at the left is Phillis Stewart Herndon. Pictured among the group are Rose Matz, Edna Roberts, Beth Scobie, Sadie Nobles, Hazel Hudson, Zoe Kimble, Bea Ziegler, Blanche Klingensmith, Suzie Crofton, Quincy Nelson, and Verna Nelson.

The bombed building pictured here represents the last dying gasp of segregation in the area. On Christmas night, 1951, a bomb exploded beneath Harry T. Moore and his wife Harriett's home in Mims, Florida. Both died as a result of the blast. No one was ever brought to justice for the murders. The Moores were killed because they fought for racial equality.

Andrew Froscher emigrated from Bavaria. He married Lavenia V. Feaster from Fesasterville, South Carolina. He bought a tract of land in LaGrange shortly after arriving in 1869 and put in an orange grove. In 1882, he received a homestead certificate, signed by President Chester A. Arthur, giving him 40 acres of land. On the plot, he built a home for his wife. They had eight children: Elbert, Carrie, Myers, May Julia, Andrew, Norris, Bertha, and Nainee. By default, Andrew became an undertaker. His fellow citizens knew that he was a good carpenter; therefore, they came to him to make coffins. Realizing there was a need for an undertaker in Titusville, he attended an embalming school in Jacksonville. He founded the first funeral home on Washington Avenue (where the Titusville City Annex is today). He also operated a downtown furniture store. He told a *Star Advocate* reporter in 1933, a few years before his death, "I never made a success of undertaking because I didn't charge enough." He sold his business to a fellow citizen, J.E. Koon. Froscher was a charter member of the Indian River Masonic Lodge, which he helped organize in 1894. He returned to Germany to visit just once, in 1905.

Captain Mills Olcott Burnham, the first permanent keeper of the Cape Canaveral Lighthouse, was an employee of the federal government and a citrus grower. When the Civil War began, the order came for the lighthouse light to be extinguished because it was thought the light might benefit the Yankee ships blockading the Confederacy. Captain Burnham carefully dismantled the light and buried the mechanism in his orange groves. After the war, he resurrected the light, which was still in excellent condition. He remained as lighthouse keeper until his death in 1886.

These costumed ladies are performing a skit. In the 1920s, they would meet weekly at Mary Pritchard's home in Titusville, and Mrs. Pritchard would assist them in preparing various programs. It was a social event for the young ladies. Pictured here, from left to right, are as follows: Dorothy Adams, Margaret Scobie, Frances Clark, Mary Pritchard, Mary Norris Froscher, and Rosamond Rogers.

This 15-year-old young man, Arthur Tresvant Feaster Jr., grew up in Brevard County, and was elected treasurer there in the 1890s.

Dr. Benjamin Rush Wilson, an early pioneer, came to North Brevard from Alabama in 1873. A practicing physician of enviable repute, he was one of the oldest and best-loved residents of the East Coast. He served as a surgeon in the Confederate Army, was grand master of Indian River Lodge # 90, mayor of Titusville, a county judge, and a Florida legislator. Also, he designed and built the city waterworks in 1896. The Wilson Home, built in 1887, is still standing at the northeast corner of Palm Avenue and Orange Street.

This was a birthday party in 1913 for Elizabeth (Beth) Scobie, who is pictured in the dark dress. Among her friends who are pictured here are the following: Pauline Parrish, Vera Wilson, Doris Crannell, Helen Crannel, Martha Tull, Mary Nobles, Buster Brown, Lester Nolle, Joe Edwards, Converse Brady, Frank Holmes, George Holmes, Mary Winterbager, Elizabeth Allen, Goldie Hopkins, Kate Thompson, Florida Berthea, and Mary Easterly.

Pictured here is Jacob B. Kyzer and his wife, Minnie R. Steele. Jake, as he was called, came with his wife from South Carolina in 1900. He became a citrus grower and also did carpentry. Their children's names were Annie, Aleph, Mitchell, Sadie, Thelma, Lillian, and Ernest.

A pioneer resident of LaGrange, Carlos Champion Curtiss was married to Joanna McCombs and was the father of silent movie star Louise Curtiss. Carlos was a purser on a St. Johns River steamboat. He and his wife homesteaded on Pine Island. Their home burned, and he sold the land and moved to LaGrange. Horse racing was a weekly event for the locals in Titusville. Carlos bet the proceeds from his farm at the races and lost it all. Their marriage, however, survived for 55 years.

Pictured here in 1920s is the Pritchard family. From left to right are as follows: (front row) W.E. Pritchard Jr. and Fanny Budge Waters; (second row) Frank T. Budge, Kate Pritchard Walker (and baby), and T. Budge Jr; (third row) Mary Boyce Pritchard, Helen Budge Wright, and Dorothy Budge McDonald; (back row) Lelia Pritchard Budge, Stella Junkin, D.B. Pritchard Sr., and Captain James Pritchard; (sitting) L.B. Walker.

This gentleman is W.C. "Kling" Klingensmith, a World War II pilot, citrus grower, cattle rancher, mayor and council member of Titusville, and a Brevard county commissioner.

In this photograph, taken around 1900, J.W. Carlile and Judge Minor S. Jones, with his daughter Elizabeth, display their kill after returning from a hunt in the piney woods of North Brevard. Deer was abundant in the area. Judge Jones was one of Florida's most colorful judges. A law passed in 1901 prohibited net fishing for mullet in the Indian River. It was particularly bad for families who were still suffering from the last crop-killing freeze. An arrest was made, and the case came before Judge Jones. The judge threw the case out, reasoning that mullet have gizzards and fowl have gizzards, therefore mullet must be fowl and not fish; therefore, the law does not apply. Hence, the local name for mullet is "Indian River chicken."

Girl Scout Troop Certificate

ISSUED BY GIRL SCOUTS, INC.

The following members of Troop Number   Two
City   Titusville   State   Florida
are registered for the year ending   February 1, 1944

Leader	Mrs. R.S. Conley	Mrs. R.Y.C. Smith
Assistant	Mrs. R.H. Sullivan	Mrs. J.J. Parrish
Assistant	Mrs. E.R. Kyzer	Mrs. Needham Bryan
Troop	Mrs. Herman Mattwood	Mrs. Durland Bennett
Committee	Mrs. Millard Smith	Mrs. Dan Belcher
		Mrs. George Nemecek

Members	Mary Jane Bennett	Carolita Rhoads
of the	Constance Bryan	Barbara Rhodes
Troop	Betty Sue Carey	Phyllis Stewart
	Carolyn Gay Conway	Vada Steburo
	Betty Lou Calder	Martha Taylor
	Elizabeth Daniels	Eunice Turner
	Joyce Lee Durden	Mary Jean Mattwood
	Nancy Ann Drea	Betty Wise
	Jean Edwards	Josephine Brown
	Martha Griner	Betty Nables
	Betty Jean Gray	
	Jean Hollis	
	Aetna May Jones	
	Norma Ruth Johnson	
	Ursula Nemecek	
	Shirley Rackels	

Juliette Low.
FOUNDER

Helen H. Means
PRESIDENT

PROGRAM: BROWNIE ☐ ; INTERMEDIATE ☒ ; SENIOR ☐ ; MARINER ☐

This February 1, 1944, Girl Scout certificate was issued to Intermediate Girl Scouts of Troop Two who had successfully completed their training. The names represent a list of "Who's Who" in the North end of Brevard County.

Mrs. J.J. Parrish Sr., affectionately know as "Miss Emma," came to Titusville in 1909 from North Carolina. She was active in community affairs. She was president of the Woman's Club and Garden Club and one of the founders of the Titusville Library. She began the Girl Scout movement in Titusville. Shortly after arriving from North Carolina, she married J.J. Parrish Sr. and raised three children in their lovely home on the banks of the Indian River. The former Florida Theater and Titusville Playhouse are named for her.

J.J. Parrish Sr. came to the area from Bowling Green, Florida, and set out early to make his mark in the citrus industry. He headed Nevins Fruit Company, Parrish Groves, and served several terms in the Florida Senate, including one as president of the Senate. Parrish Medical Center is named for him.

"STRIPES AND STARS"

-A- SUNBEAM COMEDY

with

FATTY KARR
LOUISE CURTISS
JAMES RENFROE
AND A FLOCK OF
SUNBEAM BEAUTIES.

WRITTEN & DIRECTED BY
BERT TRACY

This movie poster featured a local lady, Louise Curtiss as a star in this comedy. In this era of film making prior to the industry moving to Hollywood, Florida was a major film-producing state.

Pictured here during a dance performance on the stage in Cuba in 1929 is Sophia Miegel, a Broadway dancer who lived in Titusville. Sophia was a sister of Mrs. D.B. (Lovie) Pritchard and an aunt of Mrs. Mary Schuster. She owned a home on Riverside Drive where she taught dance to the young ladies in the area. Her home is now the residence of Attorney Hank Evans.

66

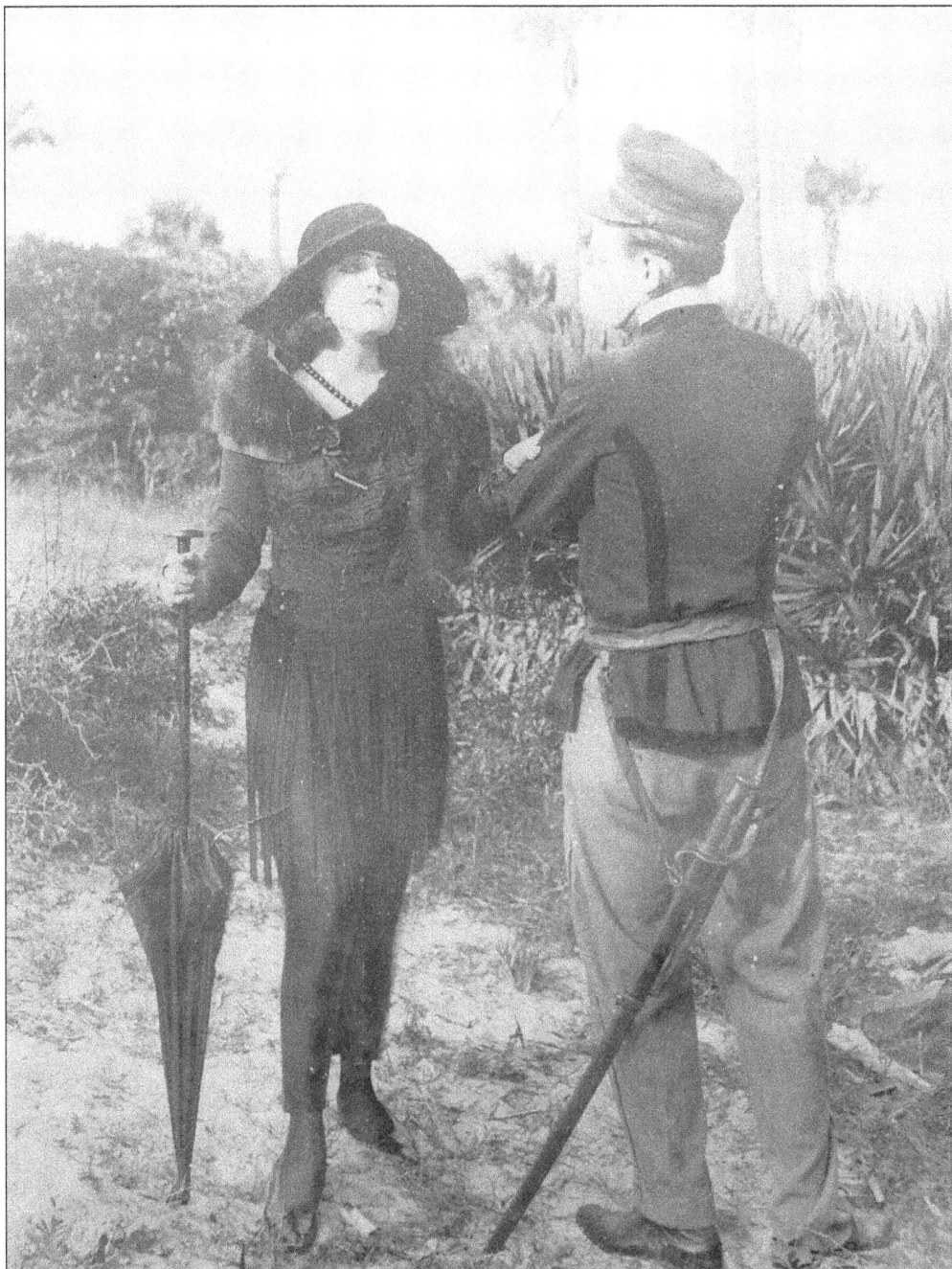

Pictured here is Titusville's own movie star, Louise Champion Curtiss, and her co-star, James Renfroe, on location in Jacksonville, Florida. Louise was a silent screen movie actress. Among her several movies, was *Stars and Stripes*, a Sunbeam Comedy. In 1919, Miss Curtiss married Otis Gray Waring and ended her movie career. They had four children who live in the county: Joanna Curtiss Titcomb, Elaine Lillian Vaughn, Lois Champion Rammage, and Champion Dyer Waring.

Brevard County sheriff, Roy Roberts, greets President Franklin Delano Roosevelt, who made a campaign whistle stop in Titusville on March 23, 1936. Roosevelt ran against the Republican nominee, Governor Alfred M. Landon of Kansas. Roosevelt, a New Deal Democrat, won one of the greatest political victories in U.S. history.

The three ladies pictured here in 1960 are participating in an installation of officers for the Order of Pythian Sisters. From left to right, they are as follows: Myrtle Thompson, Juanita Thomas Raycroft, and Jean Callins Prince.

Members of the Poinsettia Circle of the Titusville Garden Club gathered in 1958 on the lawn at the home of Roy and Edna Roberts on North Merritt Island near Orsino. From left to right, they are as follows: (standing) Zelda Cutter, Woodrow Ashcroft, unknown, unknown, Kitty Goethe, Mary Edwards, Edna Roberts, unknown, Sarah Conkling, and Hazel Hudson; (seated) Ruby Henderson, unknown, Fran Partlow, Barbara Henderson, Grace Scobie, Sophia Miegel, Mildred McVay, Trudie Nason, Joyce Rice, Kathy Rigell, and Marge Threlkeld. The man at the rear is unidentified.

Jeanette McDonald, a famed actress and soprano, is pictured here in the 1950s visiting Titusville. She is greeted with a huge bouquet of flowers by Mrs. Burton Waters, while other local women crowd around to welcome the star.

The D'Albora family gathers here for a four-generation photograph. The framed photograph is grandfather, Felix D'Albora. Members standing are John Jr. (left), baby John III (middle), and John Sr. The D'Alboras arrived in Titusville in 1923 with the Acme Fruit Company. They were wholesale distributors of produce.

Pictured here in 1950 are Walter Webb (on the left) and his son, Wally Vernon. Both men were comedians. However, at the time, it was Walter who was well known. Walter was the original "Jiggs" in the Broadway stage play Maggie and Jiggs. Comic-strip characters by the same name appeared in newspapers throughout the United States.

Traditionally, in Titusville, the losing candidates in an election were symbolically buried on Washington Avenue. The tradition began in 1928 and continued into the 1990s. The messages on the defeated candidates' graves, pictured here after the national election in 1936, are as follows: (from left to right) "Frank G. Clark, We do not want you," "Mr. Ashcat, Our deposits are guaranteed for 4 more years," and "Alf Landon and Al Smith did not help you, We want Roosevelt again."

The *Star-Advocate* newspaper in Titusville originated with the *Florida Star* in 1880 and the *Indian River Advocate* in 1890. The two papers merged in 1920. Here, publisher Henry H. Hudson, who bought the paper in 1925, presses the button for the first daily edition in 1964. He continued as publisher until his death in 1972.

Lemuel C. Crofton was a long-time attorney in Titusville who had a great interest in the history of the area, particularly the LaGrange Community Church. He served as both city and county attorney and spent several terms in the Florida Legislature. Citrus growing was his hobby.

Titusville's Centennial Celebration in 1967 featured pioneer families who joined with others to honor the city's history. Shown here in pioneer garb is Foy Duren (on the left), his sister Sadie Duren Nobles (seated at the piano), and her husband Ira (standing behind her). The Duren and Noble families were pioneers in the area. They were citrus growers, meat market operators, and fuel distributors.

The Indian River Masonic Lodge # 90, Free and Accepted Masons, was chartered on January 20, 1886, in Titusville, Florida. The fundamental purpose of Freemasonry has been to improve and strengthen the character of the individual and, through the individual, to strengthen the character of the community. The Masonic officers pictured here in 1967 strive to uphold the principles of Freemasonry. They are, from left to right, as follows: (front row) Jim Steward, Bob Moyer, Jim McCosky, Jack Dickerson, Frank Darden, and Jim Steward Jr.; (back row) Bud Hefler, Jerry Powell, Bon Murray, Gene McCosky, Jimmy Johns, unidentified, and unidentified.

The Jess Parrish Hospital Board of Trustees attended a 1964 ground-breaking ceremony for the $3.8 million, seven-story front addition to the hospital. Pictured are, from left to right, as follows: Robert Cutter, Henry Goethe, Leah Conley, Pauline Bryan, Lyle Duff, Art Wortham, and Clarence Parker.

Titusville mayor, Charles (Chuck) Morley, and his wife, Agnes, return from a public relations trip in the 1960s. It was a good will promotion by the U.S. Air Force Eastern Test Range to the city of Titusville. The Morley's owned the local Western Auto Store, and both were active in civic groups as well as politics. Agnes was a music teacher and Brevard a Library board member. Both were well known and held in the highest regard by all.

Pictured here in the 1960s with Bob Kirk, owner of Florida Wonderland, is Johnny Weissmuller. Better known to children as Tarzan of the Jungle, Weissmuller was the foremost freestyle swimmer in the world. He was associated with the theme park located at Highways 50 and U.S. 1 in Titusville.

Postmaster Phillip Crannel doffs his hat to Mayor Wendell Sease as they participate in the 1967 Titusville Centennial.

Barry Goldwater, seen here shaking hands with Barbara Kirk and standing next to Florida Congressman Lou Fry, was campaigning in the North Brevard area. Goldwater was the U.S. presidential candidate in 1964. He lost to his Democratic opponent, Lyndon B. Johnson.

Brad Davis, a 1975 Titusville High School student, became a Hollywood movie star. He starred in the feature film *Midnight Express*, a true story dramatizing an escape from a Turkish prison. His other starring roles were *Chariots of Fire*, and the television versions of *Roots*, *Robert Kennedy, His Times*, and *Sybil*.

Two prominent local men receive awards for their involvement in the coordination between NASA, the military, and the civilian population during the dramatic growth of the area in the early 1960s. As a member of the State Road Board, Max Brewer (second from the left) was the leading force behind having U.S. Highway 1 changed to four lanes and for bringing Interstate 95 through Brevard County. He was also a member of the Florida Legislature. John Nelson (far right) was the executive secretary of the East Central Florida Planning Council, worked for NASA in public relations, and was longtime executive director of the United Way in Brevard. Shown with them are (at left) Claude Wolfe, chairman of the Planning Council, and Wendell Jarrard, chairman of the Florida Development Commission.

Rory Calhoun of cowboy movie fame was associated with the Florida Wonderland theme park in Titusville during the 1960s. Those pictured here, from left to right, are as follows: H.C. Kirk (owner), Bill Walker (attorney), Randy Nunnley, Rory Calhoun (movie star), and Glenn Young (veterinarian).

Mr. Crandall Warren, a dedicated community worker and a devoted church member and officer, plans his strategy for meeting his goals as superintendent for the Missionary Baptist Church of Mims.

Chris Collinsworth was one of Astronaut High School's greatest athletes. He was state champion in the 100-yard dash, an outstanding quarterback, and an excellent basketball and baseball player. He earned a scholarship to the University of Florida, where, in his first game as a quarterback, he set a record for the longest pass completion in university history (99-yard touchdown pass). He switched to wide receiver and excelled in that position. He signed with the Cincinnati Bengals of the National Football League (NFL) and became All Pro.

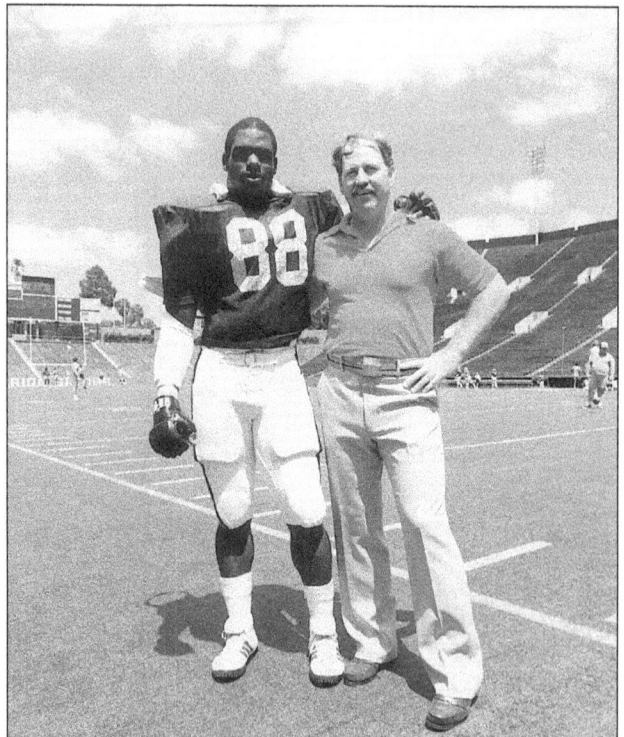

Wilbur Marshal not only made his mark in football at Astronaut High School but also as an All-American linebacker at the University of Florida and a pro football standout in the NFL. In high school, he was outstanding in football, basketball, and track. Later, he was drafted into the NFL by the Chicago Bears. He also played for the Washington Redskins, the Arizona Cardinals, and the Houston Oilers. He is shown here with his Astronaut High School coach, Jay Donnelly.

Five

EVENTS

This chapter covers a wide spectrum of life in North Brevard. For example, Doris Porter was the first woman to parachute with the 101st Airborne Division in Europe and then, at the age of 75, parachuted again. There were military patrols on the local beaches during World War II, and local men served in the military during all the wars. Musical groups provided entertainment on the streets and in the opera house. The Fourth of July was celebrated with parades and political rallies. There was an abundance of game for hunters. Bootleggers plied their illegal trade until the sheriff caught them. Titusville observed its Centennial in 1967 with a three-month celebration. NASA's space launches continue to overshadow local events and provide excitement for locals as well as thousands of tourists.

Company C, the Fifth Battalion of the Indian River Guards under the command of Captain Arthur T. Feaster are preparing to board the train for a 12-day encampment in Tallahassee. Captain Feaster, in a notice published in the April 5, 1895 *Indian River Advocate*, wishes it understood that no member may be excused, and any member disregarding this order will be dealt with severely by the court of discipline.

Leon Stewart (on the right), a soldier, is pictured here in 1917 playing cards with a fellow soldier in France during World War I. Leon survived the war and returned to Titusville, where he started and operated the East Coast Lumber Company.

This young lady, with her collie dog, is part of the war effort to raise money for the American Red Cross during World War I.

101st Airborne Division

Parachute Jumping School
United States Army
APO 472

This is to certify that:

Miss. Doris Schoedel, American Red Cross

has satisfactorily completed the special course in Parachute Packing, Ground Training and Jumping from a plane in flight. She is therefore entitled to be rated from this date,

1 March, 1944, as a qualified parachutist.

Herbert M. Sobel

Herbert M. Sobel, Capt., Ass't Commandant

In 1944, American Red Cross worker, Doris Schoedel Porter, became the first woman in the world to parachute with the 101st Airborne Division in England. However, no one had told her how to dump air from her chute, and she was dragged into a hedgerow. An officer on the ground who witnessed her landing began to chew her out until he realized she was a woman. Several years later, he wrote her to apologize. At the age of 75, and in honor of D-Day's golden anniversary, Doris repeated the event and parachuted in tandem with a local instructor here in Titusville. She has flown in a glider and plans to take a balloon flight next.

Tragedy strikes in Titusville. Due to the fear of German submarines landing spies on the local beaches during World War II, there were military patrols along the beaches. As soldiers were returning by truck from beach patrol, the truck crashed through the railing on Walker Bridge at Titusville. Six men were pinned inside the wreck and drowned. Needless to say, it was a catastrophic incident for the close knit community of Titusville.

One of Brevard's earliest musical groups was the Indian River Band of Titusville, organized in 1889. Under the directions of Will Young, the band was recognized and sought after for concerts or special events in east coast communities. Pictured here, from left to right, are as follows: (standing) Mr. Knox, Ellis Mims, Charles Williams, Carey Eloise, Ross Coleman, D.B. Pritchard, Jule Wilson, Trez Wilson, and James Pritchard; (seated) Mr. Luquestrom, Mrs. Charles Williams, Mr. Best, and Will Young.

A typical Fourth of July celebration is depicted in this Official Program of 1908. Titusville has been diligent in celebrating the Fourth of July over the last 100 years. This 1912, Fourth of July parade featured decorated wagons, bicycles, and horseback riders dressed in costumes. The paraders are passing the Julia Street intersection of Washington Avenue in Titusville. The Dixie Hotel can be seen at the end of Julia Street, and Dr. Miller's dental office is on the extreme left.

A street entertainer has the attention of this group, which is gathered on Washington Avenue, Titusville's main street, in the early 1890s. The wooden buildings shown beyond the flag pole were leveled in the 1895 fire. The brick buildings to the right survived the fire.

A Rotary float in the 1930s Fourth of July Parade passes in front of the Brevard County Courthouse.

84

Young ladies, dressed in their finery, dance around a Maypole in City Park on May Day in 1928. This was an important annual event in the lives of Titusville residents for many years. City Park (later changed to Blanton Park) was the place for gatherings every Sunday. Political rallies were held for candidates seeking public office. The whole town would gather there, and the local band would furnish music. The park had a large stage, and there were many benches placed under large oak trees with several swings to keep the youngsters busy. Ice cream was sold at the park. People came on horseback and by buggy, but most lived close enough to walk.

The City of Titusville Baseball Club of 1906 were the Florida East Coast Champions. In the early 1900s, baseball was very popular, and the games were well attended. The first baseball diamond was located west of the old ice plant on Tropic Street. Charlie Kingman was coach and manager of the team. Pictured here are, from left to right, as follows: (front row) Cowart (fielder), Carl Battle (catcher), Bert Johnson (second base), Clifford Rogero (short stop), and Tom DeCoursey (third base); (middle row) mascots; Bill Bailey, Karl Wilson, and Charlie Kingman; (back row) Charles Walker (fielder), Call Norwood (fielder), Mark McLendon (pitcher), C.B. Kingman (manager), Jess Tucker (pitcher), and Jim Revels (fielder).

The 1947 Central East Coast League pennant winning Gulls, who won the playoff against Cocoa, are shown here. Pictured, from left to right, are as follows: (front row) Buddy McBryde, Bob Lassetter, Milford Talton, Kenneth Duff, Selby Bailey, Roscoe Ray, George Whidden, and Courtland Flake; (back row) Jack Mendel, J.E. Joyner, Doug Barnhart, Harvard Cox, Smiley Wellman, Jim Blalock, Jim Covello, Bob Hartman, and William Levan. David Marese is the bat boy in front.

The order of Pythian Sisters was organized at Warsaw, Indiana, on October 22, 1888. The independent auxiliary of the Knights of Pythias, Titusville Temple #22, was instituted April 6, 1910. Among the sisters pictured here in the 1970s are Jettie Cottrell (in the front with rose), Inez Futch, Francis Raynor, and Juanita Thomas Raycroft.

These Boy Scouts belonged to Troop 320 in Titusville. The scouts in this 1955 ceremony, from left to right, are as follows: John (Ziggy) Olewski, unidentified, Ed Wager, Karl Lee Thorne, Donald Wager, Bunny Parrish, Randy Ziegler, Ronnie Bohannon, Bernard Taylor, unidentified, and Bobby Brown.

Girl Scout Troops and programs have been popular over the decades in North Brevard. Leaders of this troop were Eleanor Smith (left) and Virginia Swink (right). Troop members were, from left to right, as follows: (first row) Katrina Linquist, Saralyn Higgs, Bennie Jo Lee, Jeanette Taylor, and Phyllis Wilson; (second row) Mary Jane Revels, Carol Smith, Shirley Kyser, Lynn Shuler, and unknown; (third row) unknown, Pat Christie, Enid Taylor, Billie Ann Folsom, Mary Lee Hall, and Dorothy Hall.

Sheriff Roy Roberts poses with the remnants of boot-leg liquor still that he has just destroyed. He is holding the kettle, or cooker, and the coil is on the ground at the left rear bumper. During prohibition, there was very little enforcement of an unpopular federal law. Afterwards, when there was a tax to be collected on whiskey, enforcement became profitable for the local governments.

The July 21, 1916 *East Coast Advocate* newspaper in Titusville described how a lead-lined box was placed in the cornerstone of Titusville School, which was the first concrete school built in Titusville. Though well built, the school was razed in 1967 to make way for a new city hall. Here, the cornerstone is opened by Titusville Mayor Wendell Sease. Examining a copy of the *Star-Advocate* Newspaper is publisher, Henry H. Hudson, and editor, Bob Hudson. The cornerstone and its contents are currently on display at the North Brevard Historical Museum.

This "locomotive" was built by E.B. Pirtle for the Lion's Club. Here, in 1950, it leaves on a 20-day, 5000-mile journey to Mexico City. While at the Lion's Convention, it won a $750 prize for best float in the parade. The "locomotive" was in great demand for parades.

Daughters of the American Revolution gathered at Mrs. Mary (Beth) Scobie's home to celebrate the Titusville Centennial in 1967. Among those pictured are Emma Henderson, Eula Miley, Beth Scobie, Saidee Nobles, Minnie Williams, Elizabeth Bradley, and Florence Bell.

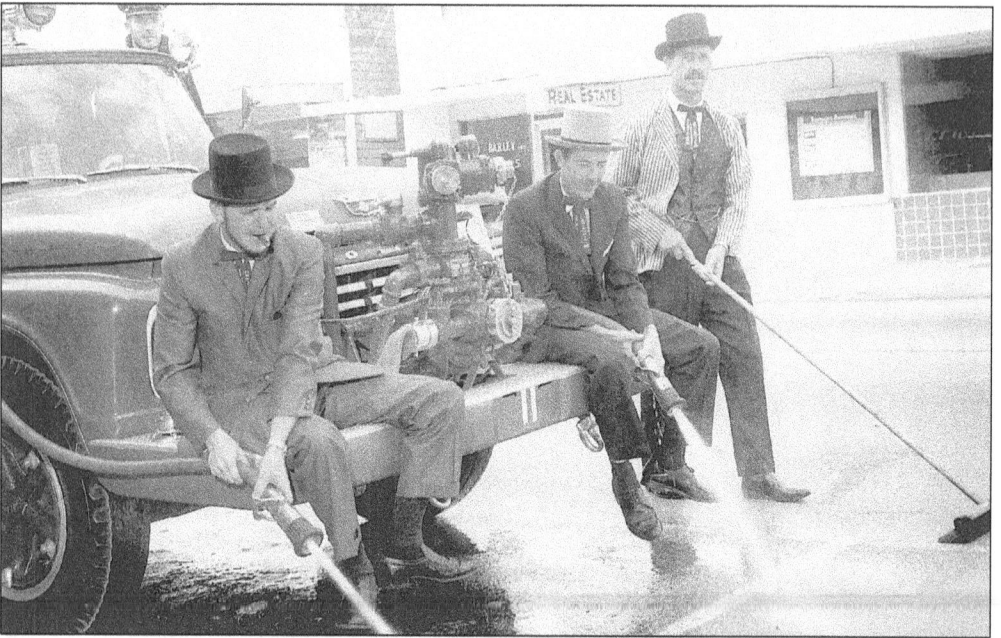

During the 1967 Titusville Centennial, lots of help was needed to get the city shipshape. Pictured here, providing questionable help, are the following, from left to right: Mayor Wendell Sease, Councilmen John Gandy, and Vern Jansen.

Titusville, gateway to the Moon Port at Kennedy Space Center, was the ideal location for viewing the early missile launches. This 1972 launch, like many others, attracted viewers, who came prepared in autos, campers, and tents, willing to stay through expected launch delays. In the heyday of moon launches, one quarter of a million people crowded along the shores of the Indian River to view the historic launches. Every available spot was taken for watching the launches. Here, watching the Apollo 16 lift-off in 1972, campers line the shore, as people jockey for every inch of space, including space on the Indian River.

Six

TRANSPORTATION
LAND, WATER, AND AIR

Throughout history, towns and cities have been established along waterways and later railroad lines. At the northern end of the Indian River, early settlers established the town of LaGrange and Sand Point (now Titusville). The Haulover was a narrow strip of land between the Mosquito Lagoon and the Indian River. Boats and goods had to be dragged across the land until a canal was dug. Then came the railroads, first connecting North Brevard with the St. Johns River at Lake Monroe near Sanford. Next, Henry Flagler extended his rail line south from Jacksonville. The first roads generally followed the paths of the first pioneers on horseback or in wagons. Early automobiles and trucks used these same well-worn paths. Eventually, the state began road building, followed by the federal government. North-south and east-west roads connected all points of Brevard with the rest of the state. In 1928, the first airport was constructed in Titusville and is now known as Dunn Airpark. It was for private planes and never developed commercially. In the late 1930s, Titusville and Cocoa combined to build TiCo Airport South of Titusville. During World War II, it served as a Naval training base. The airport is being expanded to attract more commercial business.

This stretch of sand was known as Cheney Highway and was named for an Orlando mayor. For Brevard residents wishing to travel west from Indian River City to Orlando, this trail of sand through the St. Johns Prairie was 28 miles of bad news. While it was possible to negotiate the deep sand with the automobiles and trucks of the early 1920s, wagons pulled by mules and oxen fared much better.

These men and vehicles in the 1920s, are part of the road building crew that built the road from Titusville to the St. Johns River. Eventually, the road known as Cheney Highway became Highway 50 and was completed across the state to the Gulf.

This 5-ton white truck was a road department truck. Although slow, with a chain drive, it was very powerful and capable of carrying heavy loads over rough terrain.

Frank Snell, manager of the Titusville Coca-Cola Bottling Company, with his 5-year-old daughter, Waldene, readies this truck for deliveries to local stores in 1929.

Lawrence Jepson, Frank Smith, J.E. MooMaw, and an unknown passenger are riding in style here in 1920s, on the Dixie Highway, the main thoroughfare between Jacksonville and Miami, through Titusville.

These men pose beside the first automobile to cross the new Walker Bridge. The bridge, built in 1922, connected Merritt Island with the mainland at Titusville. The Hotel Dixie and the Titus House are in the background.

The Fulford Bus Line is seen here unloading passengers at Clark's Corner. A bus service from points west, Orlando and Tampa, connected with North/South buses along Dixie Highway.

The moving of houses or other buildings in the early 1900s was best done by oxen power, as shown here in Indian River City when Harry Sisson (Sisson Road in Titusville is named for him.) and Dolph Nelson decided to move this structure from their farm into town.

Why would these women leave the safety and security of their homes to live in a tent? These women are part of a once select group of adventurers referred to as Tin Can Tourists. After World War I, with the advent of cheap automobiles (Tin Lizzie) and a yen to seek adventure, people hit the road. There were no tourist courts or motels. A tent was the cheapest way to provide shelter and was easily stored in the vehicle. The Tin Can Tourist association was formed in Tampa, Florida, in 1919.

In the 1960s, the bridge over the St. Johns River on State Road 46 was under construction. The area suffered a freeze, and a lot of citrus was quickly picked and trucked to juice processing plants in Central Florida. To help in this effort, the state government lifted weight restrictions on most Florida bridges, among them this wooden-decked bridge. The trailer-truck load was too much, and it partially broke through. A dangerous task is performed by workers in the boat under the truck as they try to open a gate and dump the oranges. After attempts to lift it by drag lines and cranes failed, the men in the boat unlocked the tailgate, and the fruit rolled into the river. Fishermen in nearby boats started picking up the fruit, and at least two boats became overloaded and sank.

On his 63rd birthday, July 31, 1926, Henry Ford revealed to the public his Ford Flivver airplane, designed by 27-year-old Ford engineer Otto C. Koppen. The plane had a 20-foot wingspan, weighing 320 pounds, and could cruise at 100 m.p.h. It was a single low-wing monoplane with a 40-horsepower, all-magnesium engine. The test pilot was a close friend of Ford's, Harry Brooks. The plane, powered by a Ford engine and produced in the Ford factory, had great promise of being a mass-produced, low-cost aircraft. Brooks was assigned to make a publicity tour of Florida and build up experience on the model. Brooks made an unscheduled landing at Titusville Beach, where local citizens meet with the pilot. At left is Roy Roberts Sr., and Ira Nobles. Behind the pilot, wearing the hat with a brim is J.W. Hanson, Star Advocate news editor. Brooks took off flying south along the east coast only to crash into the sea and drown off Melbourne Beach on February 2, 1928.

The good ship *Sylph* ferries these young ladies over the Indian River to visit with friends in the 1920s.

This group of men and hunting dogs are aboard their boat, *Leo*, and are putting in at the Salt Lake Landing. They are returning from a trip on the St Johns River.

The steamboat *Narmerka*, traversed the Haulover Canal, which linked the Mosquito Lagoon on the east to the Indian River on the west. For 300 years, the American Indians of the area hauled their canoes across a narrow strip of land between the two bodies of water. The American Indians, and later the pioneer settlers, covered the ground with stripped bark from mulberry tree and slid the boats over the slick surface of the bark. In some instances, goods were carried across the land on the backs of slaves. In fact, slaves owned by a citrus grower on Merritt Island dug the first canal.

The paddle-wheel steamboat *Swan* plied the waters of the Indian River and made regular stops at Titusville, carrying passengers and freight.

Pineapples are not easily bruised or quick to spoil; therefore, they can be shipped long distances. Here, in the early 1920s, this sailboat moves pineapples to northern markets.

On February 21, 1908, this passenger train traveling through Titusville crashed into the rear of a freight train. Luckily, there were no injuries.

An excursion train on the Jacksonville, Tampa and Key West Railroad, known as the JT and KW, ran a branch line from Enterprise to Titusville. It was a happy day when the train connected the steamboat traffic on the St. Johns River with the Indian River in 1885. The tracks ran down Broad Street to the docks. The depot was where the Baldwin shopping center is now located. President Cleveland had the train stop at an orange grove where his wife climbed a ladder to pick fruit.

In 1925, with good highways still to be built and trucks mostly used to haul local goods, most local shipments of freight out of Titusville were by rail. The freight waiting on the station platform of this Florida East Coast railway station is typical of the type and amount shipped daily. The Brevard County Courthouse is undergoing extensive renovations at the rear of the station.

100

With rough terrain and no paved roads in the area, this 1920s garage in Indian River City was kept busy repairing local automobiles.

Engine 592 in 1907 served as a donkey engine and shuttled freight cars back and forth to the main line. They were loaded in the yard of the Titusville Lumber Company.

Transportation is where you find it. For children who like to dream of being a fireman, fire trucks provide the best kind of ride. Here, Chief James Brown gives a thrilling ride to lots of children.

Horseless age in the South.

Oxen were more docile and not as ornery as mules nor as highly strung as horses. They were ideal for pulling heavy loads over rough terrain. Here, a turpentine wagon, which has collected sap buckets from the tapped pine trees, is now taking the sap to a still to be distilled into turpentine and other by-products.

Seven

WATERWAYS AND BEACHES

This area is blessed with many navigable bodies of water including the Atlantic Ocean. North Brevard stretched westward from the beaches to the St. Johns River, but the major transportation was on the Indian River. The northern end of Banana River and Banana Creek were also much used waterways. The lakes, rivers, and ocean were sources for fishing and water-related activities. Boat building and commercial fishing were early industries in North Brevard, and after the bridge was built at Titusville in the early 1920s to span the Indian River, Playalinda, Titusville, and Desota Beaches grew in popularity. The building of a pier at Cape Canaveral enabled shrimp and fishing boats to unload their catch. The construction of Port Canaveral paved the way for large freighters to use the facility to serve the growing needs of Central Florida. In more recent years, the port has become home to cruise ships.

Mr. George Quarterman, who was the last person to man the lighthouse, and his wife stand in front of the U.S. Coast Guard Station, which was located at Titusville Beach near the Canaveral Club. It was know as the Chester Shoals Station. It was in operation for many decades, providing search and rescue service from World War I through World War II.

Canaveral Light House, Titusville, Fla.

The Cape Canaveral Lighthouse was first erected in 1847 as a navigational aid to prevent ships from running aground on the hazardous Cape shoreline. Originally, it was 60 feet tall, made of brick, and the lamp burned whale oil. A newer and taller lighthouse was built of wood in 1868. Eventually, more permanent materials, metal and brick, were used. The Civil War caused a blackout of the light. After the war, Captain Miles O. Burnham resurrected the light equipment from its hiding place in his citrus grove. The present structure is 168 feet tall, and the light can be seen for ten miles at sea. The lighthouse was automated in the 1950s, at which time the last keeper, Captain Floyd Quarterman, retired. Although accessible only by boat and later by a shell road from the south, it was once a thriving community with a post office, pier, hotel, schoolhouse, and homes. Unfortunately, the lighthouse is no longer accessible to the public since it has become a part of the Cape Canaveral Air Force Station, where missiles are launched.

Mr. Woodward, the "Sailing Photographer," took care of the photographic needs of Brevard from 1888 to 1910. Mr. Woodward and his family lived aboard this floating photographic studio, as he traveled the Indian River and other waterways, taking and developing photographs. Many of the photographs used in this publication were taken by Woodward.

This is Quarter Boat No. 2, for the Florida East Coast Railroad. When Henry Flagler, the railroad czar, was building his railroad down Florida's East Coast, there was no housing available for his workers. He brought in this quarter boat barge to house his workers. As the railroad extended southward, the quarter boat would also be moved.

Lorillard Boat Company, established in 1906, was the first boat builder in Titusville. Located on the Indian River between Broad and Main Streets, they specialized in small fishing boats. This is the famous P. Lorillard Company of the tobacco industry.

In 1942, during World War II, the Correct Craft Boat Company negotiated a 60-year lease for a manufacturing facility at the Titusville Yacht Basin. They built small landing crafts for the Army and ship tenders for the Navy. Correct Craft was known for its high performance speed boats such as those used at the Florida Attraction, Cypress Gardens. Nelson Marina took over the marina lease in 1960.

These families brought their autos over from the mainland by boat. Having only rutted axle-deep sand roads on the mainland, these wide, packed beaches were an inviting place for drivers and beach-goers.

106

Net fishing was a profitable enterprise in the Indian River Lagoon. When the railroad came, it so advanced the progress of commercial fishing that, in 1895, it was described as a factor in the fish supply of the United States.

In 1910, prior to catch limits, bass were abundant. Here, three fishermen display their 2,200 pounds of largemouth bass caught on cane poles in the span of one week. The reader today must keep in mind that there was no refrigeration available for these fish. The fishermen, from left to right, are Fred Bradley, Bill Raulerson, and Joseph Bradley. The bass, some weighing as much as 14 pounds, were caught in Puzzle Lake, which is a part of the St. Johns River.

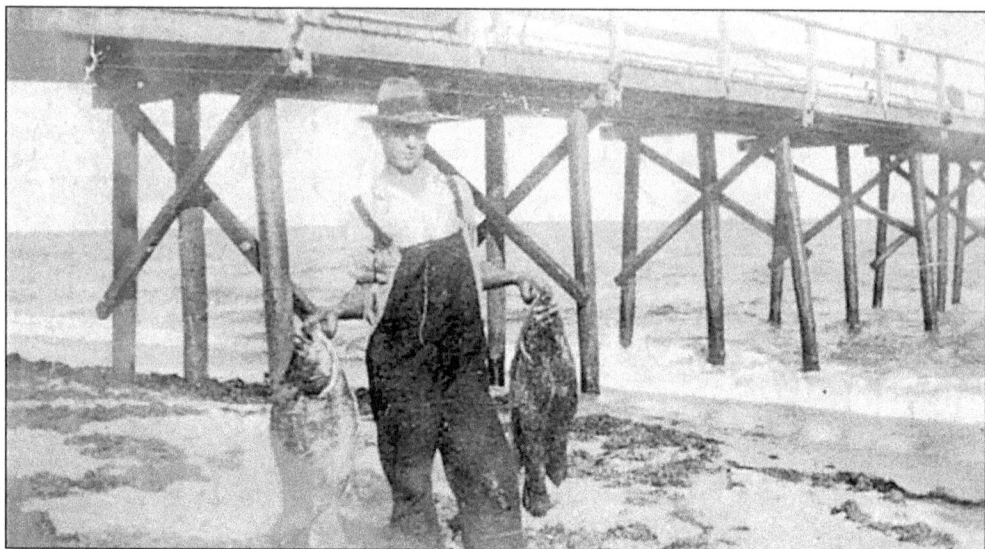

Elliott Myer Burns displays the day's catch, caught from the Canaveral Pier in the background. The pier, built in the early 1900s, was a favorite fishing spot. However, it, too, disappeared as missile launch pads took over the area.

One of the most popular fishing camps in North Brevard was the Beacon 42 Fish Camp, near Allenhurst, on the shores of the Mosquito Lagoon. Here, the owner, Ed McCormick, displays his catch of the day.

This concrete bridge was opened in 1948. It connected Titusville with North Merritt Island. In the late 1930s, fill was pumped in for a causeway and a steel and concrete bridge was begun; however, World War II caused a shortage of steel, and work on the bridge stopped. It was not until 1948 that the new concrete and steel bridge was completed. The fishing pier, shown alongside the new bridge, is the remnants of the old wooden bridge that was built in 1922. It is a popular place for fishermen.

This raised draw bridge over the Haulover Canal is a far cry from the original wooden bridge that spanned the 3-foot-deep, 14-foot-wide canal of the 1850s. This concrete and steel span, built in the 1950s, replaced the swing bridge seen at the right. The bridge in the up position causes a bottleneck for missile workers. However, boat traffic has the right-of-way.

Manatees are a protected species. However, this was not always true, and because of their harmless and docile nature, they were abused and misused until their numbers reached the point of almost becoming extinct. This manatee in the 1960s was being captured for use in a local tourist attraction.

There are many ways to enjoy the bodies of water in the area. The annual Indian River Festival has been an event in April for many years in Titusville. One of the highlights of the four-day event is the Big Raft Race held on the waters of the Indian River. Here, the Jess Parrish Memorial Hospital raft, named the USS Bed Pan, competes. Entries are from businesses, clubs, and individuals.

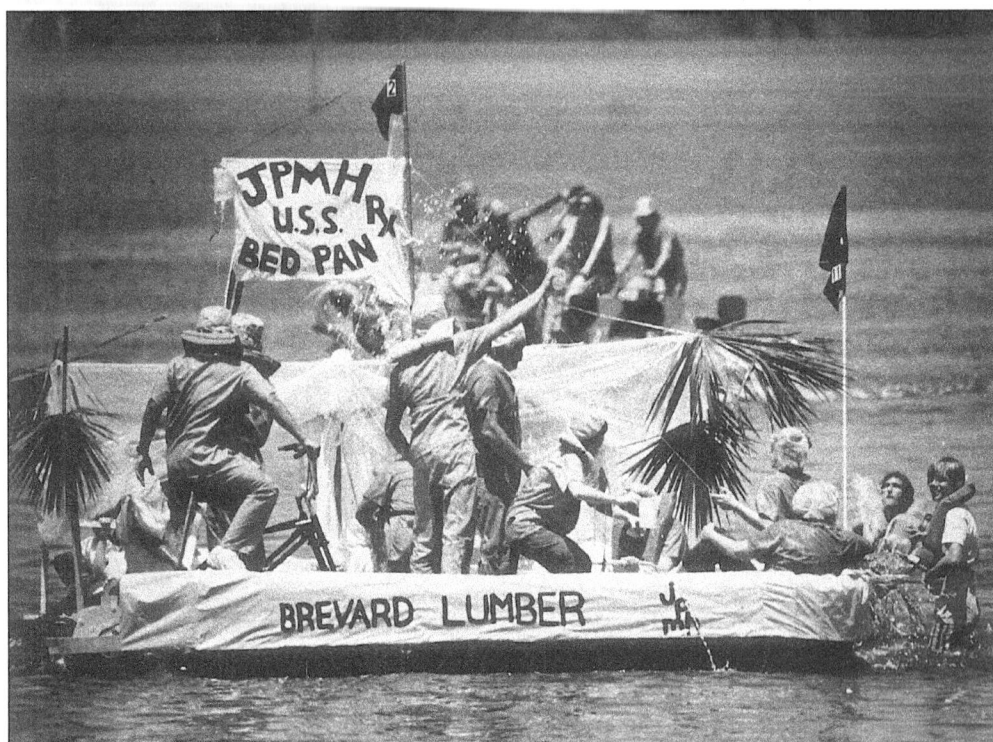

Eight

CITRUS AND
AGRICULTURE

The famed Indian River citrus country begins in North Brevard and stretches south along the Indian River. It was just east of Titusville on North Merritt Island that Douglas Dummitt planted the first citrus trees in the area. By 1867, it was reputed to be the largest grove in Florida, containing 1,700 trees. Unlike many others in the state, his grove survived several devastating freezes. Budwood from these trees was used to start many other groves in the Indian River area. Thus, citrus for many decades has been the major agriculture crop in North Brevard. It spawned the planting of thousands of acres of trees, the construction of packing houses, and the establishment of retail fruit stands along the highways.

Other agricultural products were successfully grown in the area. Celery was successfully grown west of Indian River City and Mims. Pineapples were grown in Titusville and North Merritt Island. Saw palmetto berries were harvested for medicine, and palmetto branches are still harvested for shipment to the Palm Sunday market. Wild saw grass was harvested for broom construction. Sugar cane was a popular crop yielding many types of sweets. Papayas, guavas, and mangoes were common throughout the area. Lettuce, cabbage, carrots, and other commercial produce were grown in large quantities.

The *Indian River Advocate* of Nov. 20, 1896, reported in the social column that, "The annual sugar cane grinding at Mr. Peter Raulerson's is now in operation. This is the latest most important feature of the season and has been looked forward to with delight by both children and grownup people. It has been largely attended, not only by home folks, but by a number of visitors from other places, all partaking of the childish joy of drinking the juice, and scraping candy from the kettle with little paddles. Many thanks are due Mr. & Mrs. Raulerson for the pleasant time." Sugar cane can grow to a height of 18 feet and is harvested in eight months.

Employees pose for a photograph in 1902 at the Nole, Brockett and Parrish Packing House of Mims. In 1928, it was purchased by the Mims Citrus Growers Association. Prior to the railroad, fruit was shipped by steamer to northern markets. Transportation to and from the groves was via horse-drawn carts. Until the railroads came, fruit was shipped in barrels via steamboat on the St Johns River.

The Rotary Club of Titusville has filled this boxcar with produce, which is destined for the drought-ravaged Midwest of the 1930s. Pictured are, from left to right, as follows: unidentified, J.J. Parrish, W.F. Darden, Dr. J.C. Spell, J.D. Nash Sr., and Benjamin R. Gorgas. Mr Gorgas, a horticulturist, owned the farm where most of the produce was grown.

112

These barrels were manufactured in the Scobie Supply Company of Titusville. Here, in 1906, at the Florida East Coast station, the barrels, used for shipping produce, citrus fruit, and fish to northern markets, have been loaded on a flatcar. Ice was placed in the barrels so the fish would not spoil. Oranges survived better if they were individually wrapped in tissue paper prior to shipping. This factory produced barrels for 50 years and burned in the 1960s.

A 1950s view inside Clark's "A-Head" brand citrus packing plant in Indian River City. Citrus boxes move overhead on a conveyor belt ready to be filled with Indian River fruit.

Orange pickers in 1910, stop to pose for a photograph. The baskets used to gather the oranges could weigh 100 pounds. Heavy clothing was worn by the pickers because of the thorns on the citrus trees.

This orange picker uses a bag, which was an improvement over the woven baskets previously used by pickers. The laborers were paid by the box, which they filled from their bags. Many of the pickers were imported from Mexico.

This Nevins Fruit Company label of Indian River fruits was recognized by households throughout the country as providing a quality product. Packing houses belonged to an association that set high standards for grading and shipping any fruit carrying the Indian River label.

The Brevard Packing Company, located on Route 46 in Mims and shown here in 1926, carried the Blue Goose Label.

The Nevins Fruit Company, on the main line of the Florida East Coast Railway, is still in operation today.

A large steam-powered dredge, in 1912, digs the Addison Canal. The canal was needed to drain the land for agricultural pursuits. Citrus groves require well-drained soil.

116

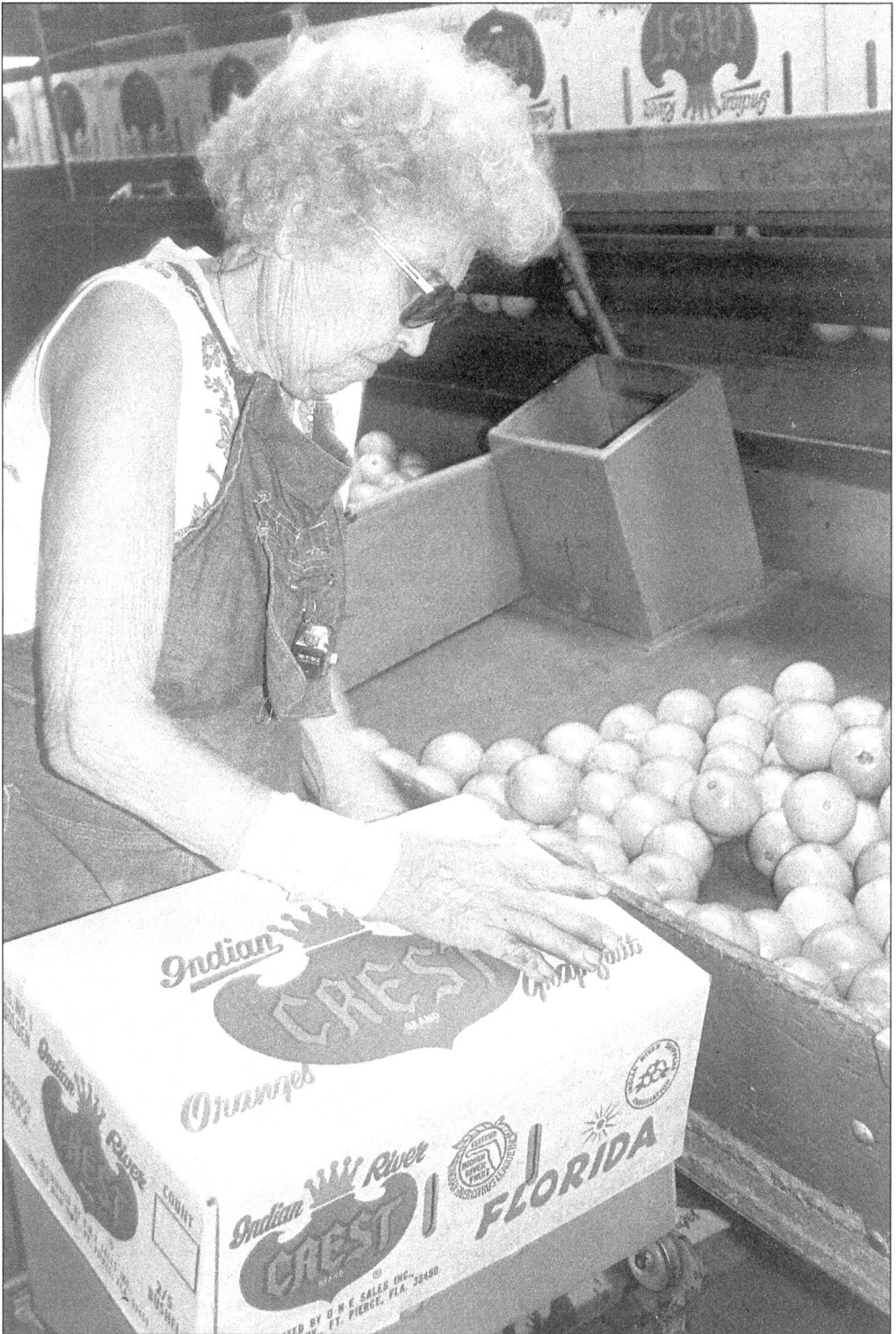

Mrs. Lizzie Nolle, shown here closing a box of navel oranges in 1972, had completed 34 years as a fruit grader and packer. She was employed by the Nevins Fruit Company of Mims.

Pictured here is a young citrus grove in the 1920s planted by Roy Roberts on Merritt Island. The grove is still in existence even though the John F. Kennedy Space Center now occupies the area. The groves in some cases are leased back to the grower, and the growers are responsible for cultivating and gathering the fruit. Australian pines were planted at the edge of the groves to protect the trees from freezes. However, in 1983, a severe freeze hit the area and killed most of the Australian pines and devastated the citrus crop.

In 1910, these workers cultivate a pineapple field in Titusville. At the turn of the century, the largest cash crop in Brevard County was pineapple. The pineapple plant is in the bromeliad or air plant family. Its cupped leaves are able to store water. During the 1920s, a severe freeze coupled with the importation of cheap Cuban pineapples ended most of the pineapple growing in the county.

These saw palmetto berry drying racks were a major source of income for Robert (Bob) Cleveland Burns, on North Merritt Island, in the 1930s. Today, most males over 60 years of age will have heard of these berries and their use for prostate problems. The pioneer white man learned of the many medicinal uses for the saw palmetto from the North American Indians, who used saw palmetto berries as a general tonic to nourish the body, to improve appetite, and to remedy impotence, low libido, and urinary problems. The saw palmetto is a small palm tree with large leaves and deep red to black berries.

This Titusville State Market was built in 1936 by the Work Programs Administration (WPA). It was built of native coquina that was mined locally. The market was a particularly popular place on Saturdays when local farmers brought their farm products to be sold. The building once housed the Titusville Chamber of Commerce and vehicle tag agency. Later, it was used as a tourist club meeting headquarters, a recreation center, and a library.

119

In 1953, after a hard, hot summer day, Lawrence Bishop stands in front of his farm building between two papaya trees. He farmed and cultivated citrus groves but was known for having the best papaya fruit in North Brevard.

Here, field workers harvest celery west of the Indian River in the 1920s. Celery was grown near what is now the Bent Oak Golf and Country Club. However, due to depletion of the soil, celery growing and most vegetable growing was moved west of the St. Johns River near Sanford.

Nine

PLACES IN THE PAST

One hundred years ago, on a strip of land between the Indian and Banana Rivers, lay a spit of land called North Merritt Island. Here, pioneer settlers came to begin a new life among the palmetto thickets, mosquitoes, rattlesnakes, alligators, and the best fishing in the United States. Early settlers built crude palmetto thatched huts and later improved them with logs. At best, they were primitive dwellings. Nevertheless, these were the people that formed the nucellus of 17 settlements, towns, and communities that, today, exist only in the memories of older Brevard residents. In the 1960s, the U.S. Government acquired 87,000 acres on North Merritt Island, costing $55 million. This was done to provide a safe launch and fall-back area for the missile industry.

The honor roll of former towns and communities, in most cases, bears the name of the first land owner to move into the area: Allenhurst, Wilson, Orsino, Mortonhurst, and Clifton. Other names describe a map location: Wisconsin Village, Shiloh, Haulover, Heath, Eldora, Playalinda Beach, Titusville Beach, and a place called Happy Creek, located where else but next to Happy Hammock. Prior to the Merritt Island uprooting, there had been an earlier displacement of people in the 1950s, when the government took the land for the Cape Canaveral Missile Test Center. There were places called Canaveral Beach, Artesia, Chester Shoals, and DeSota Beach.

Visionaries, prior to the government takeover, had development plans for other places that never quite succeeded: Satellite Estates, Myrtle Park Shoals, Paradise Bay, Dummitt Plantation Estates, Tween Seas Isle, Anna-Myrt Island, and Canaveral Harbor, the city of romance.

Like former owners and their property, many photographs of these long ago places have disappeared. The following photographs are offered in an attempt to regain the essence of an era that exists only in the fading memories of an elderly few.

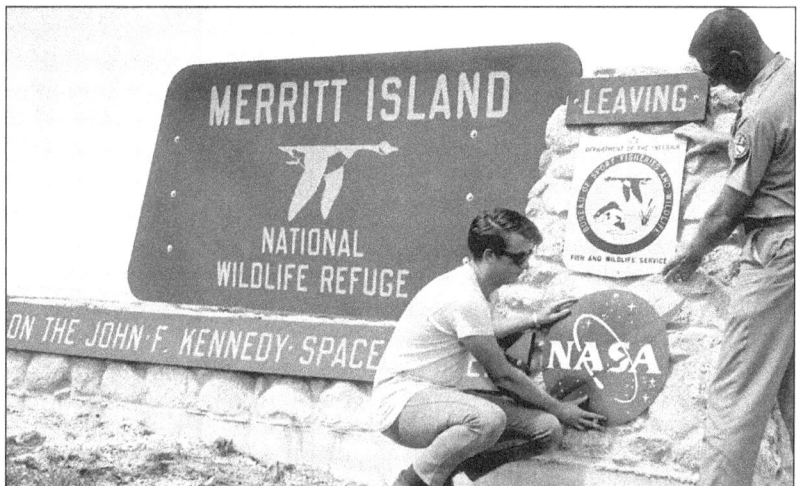

The message on this sign, "leaving," tells it all. Towns that were home to many people are long gone, displaced by the Merritt Island Wildlife Refuge or The John F. Kennedy Space Center.

The first inhabitants of North Brevard County were the Paleo Indians, descendants of the ancient people that crossed the land bridge between Asia and Alaska some 30,000 years ago. They are the ancestors of the modern American Indians. The 1984–86 Windover Archeological Dig provided a look at the past, where the 7,000-year-old intact remains of 169 Aboriginal Americans were discovered. Amazingly, there were 90 intact human brains, which continue to provide a wealth of information for researchers.

Once located on the north side of Haulover Canal, Allenhurst was one of the towns displaced by NASA's takeover of the area. It was the center of sports fishing on North Merritt Island. Pictured here, at the Allenhurst Post Office in 1901, is longtime resident Mr. J. Allen with a friend and a curious mule.

This home, although built on raised pilings, is perilously close to being inundated by water. The toppled tree to the right was a tall pine that blew down during the night, just missing the house. Not much of a house, however, it was the original home of the Roberts family. It withstood the ravages of the elements such as this hurricane in 1926, which devastated Merritt Island. This home was later replaced with a two-story, coquina rock home. Nevertheless, it could not withstand progress and fell to the axe of the government.

Barbara Smith, granddaughter of the founder of Orsino, had to be ever vigilant when traveling the sand trails of Merritt Island. Here, she is holding a deadly rattlesnake in one hand and the shotgun she used to kill it in the other.

Mr. Walton's two daughters are sitting in his new 1912 Cadillac, which was the first automobile in the Allenhurst community of Merritt Island. It was brought in by boat because there was no bridge at the time.

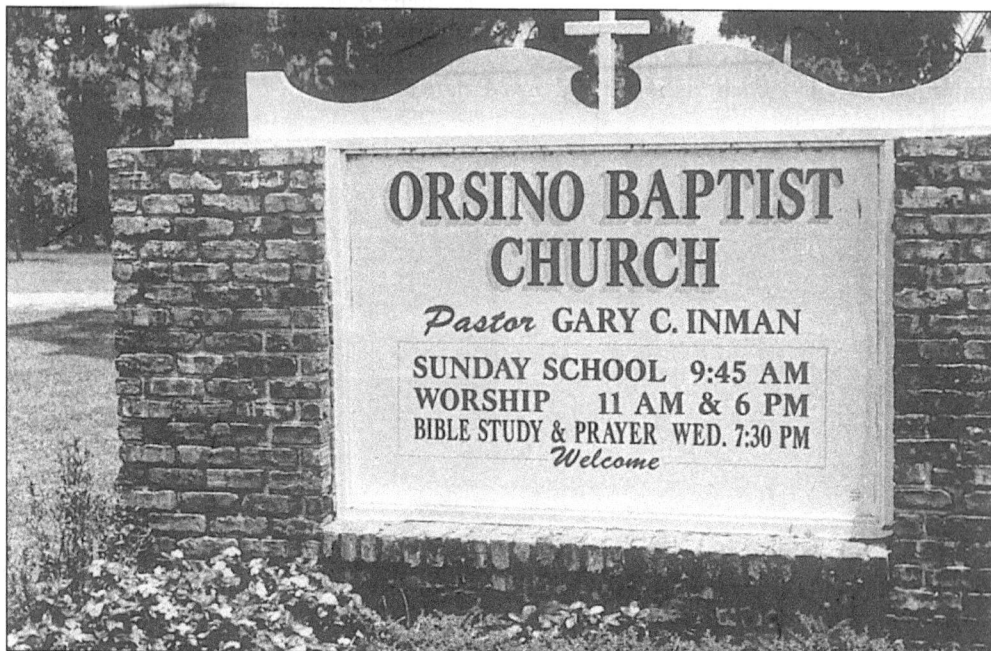

Orsino Baptist Church is the last remains of a community named for Orsino Smith, the town's first postmaster. Much of the previous community and home sites were incorporated into NASA's missile launch complex.

The Harvard or Boston Club, later known as the Canaveral Club, was a rich man's Utopia, surrounded by desolate, mosquito-infested marshland. The 20-room clubhouse was started by some of the richest young men in Boston. They were graduates of Harvard's class of 1890. Membership was limited to 14, and it required a $5,000 membership fee. At least two presidents, Grover Cleveland and Benjamin Harrison, were guests during the winter hunting season. Kennedy Space Center's Launch Pad 39 now occupies the area.

Shiloh Community Center was built by residents of North Merritt Island in 1934. It served as a meeting hall, school building, and church for several decades. Like other communities on Merritt Island, it fell to the bulldozers as Kennedy Space Center came into existence.

In 1925, an attempt was made to raise capital by selling stock in the proposed Orsino Telephone, Telegraph & Power company. It is not known if any stocks were sold. However, the residents had to continue with their oil lamps because the plant never materialized.

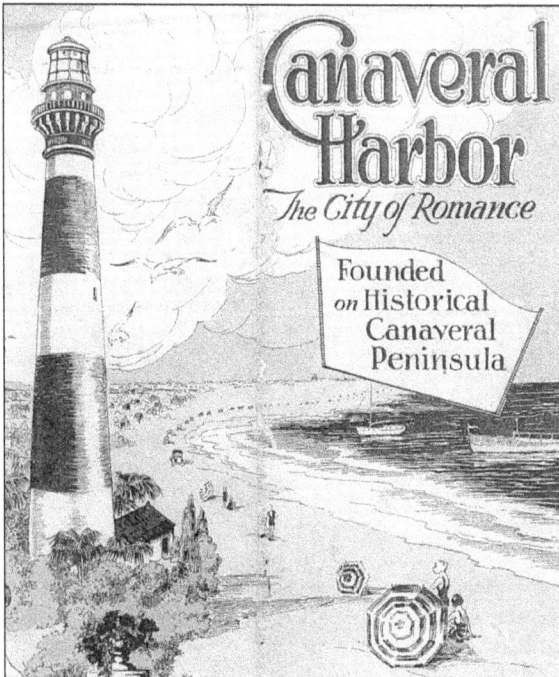

The "City of Romance," a 1920s sales brochure for Canaveral Harbor, asks potential investors to visualize an area that would surpass Miami Beach. The comparison pitch was that both were on the Atlantic Ocean and lay east of the Dixie Highway. There, the similarity ended, because Canaveral Harbor would soon take its place as one of the leading seaports of the South. Canaveral Harbor was slated for greatness. Nothing ever came of the "City of Romance." Greatness did come, however, to the area some 30 years later, after the launch of the first U.S. satellite into space, which paved the way for future space travel. Canaveral Harbor, or as it is now called, Port Canaveral, has become a launch site for millions of tourists.

The Roy Roberts family home, which was located until the 1960s near the town of Orsino on Merritt Island, passes in defeat before the gigantic Vertical Assembly Building at the Kennedy Space Center on Merritt Island. The Roberts homesteaded the land and eventually replaced their first home with this two-story, coquina structure. It was relocated by son Roy to Scottsmoor, where he still resides.

Local citizens visit the NASA Crawler, which travels the roadway from the Vertical Assembly Building to the pad, carrying shuttles to be launched into space. Many of the local citizens are employed at the space center, which has displaced the citrus growers, farmers, and merchants.

Cape Canaveral Florida

These Cape Canaveral missile launch facilities, now known as the Air Force Eastern Test Range, occupy the sites of former communities such as Canaveral Beach, Artesia, Chester Shoals, and Desota Beach. It was from here in the 1950s that the Army Ballistic Missile Agency placed the first United States satellite in orbit. Additionally, the first man to orbit the earth was launched from here.